TRIBE AND STATE IN ASIA THROUGH TWENTY-FIVE CENTURIES

Sumit Guha

ASIA
SHORTS

Published by the Association for Asian Studies
Asia Shorts, Number 10
www.asianstudies.org

Published by Association for Asian Studies, 825 Victors Way, Suite 310, Ann Arbor, MI 48108 USA

Cover image: A Bhil hunter with a flare, helping a hunter with a bow to hunt deer at night. Source: https://commons.wikimedia.org/wiki/File:A_Bhil_hunter_with_a_flare,_helping_a_hunter_with_a_bow_to_hunt_deer_at_night_(6125080998).jpg

Cheshire Cat image: https://commons.wikimedia.org/wiki/File:Alice_par_John_Tenniel_24.png

Cataloging-in-Publication Data is available from the Library of Congress.

Tribe and State in Asia through Twenty-Five Centuries

ASIA
SHORTS

"ASIA SHORTS" offers concise, engagingly-written titles written by highly-qualified authors on topics of significance in Asian studies. Topics are intended to be substantive, generate discussion and debate within the field, and attract interest beyond it.

The AAS is exploring new ways of making rigorous, timely, and accessible work by scholars in the field available to a wide audience of informed readers. This new series complements and leverages the success of the pedagogically-oriented AAS series, "Key Issues in Asian Studies" and is designed to engage broad audiences with up-to-date scholarship on important topics in Asian studies.

"Asia Shorts" books:

- Have a clear point of view, a well-defined, and even provocative argument rooted in a strong base of evidence and current scholarship.

- Are written in an accessible, jargon-free style suitable for non-specialist audiences.

- Are written by a single author or a small group of authors (scholars, journalists, or policymakers).

- Are rigorously peer reviewed.

For further information, visit the AAS website: www.asianstudies.org

AAS books are distributed by Columbia University Press.

For orders or inquiries, please visit https://cup.columbia.edu

COLUMBIA
UNIVERSITY
PRESS

ABOUT THE AUTHOR

Sumit Guha is Professor of History at the University of Texas at Austin. He was born in New Delhi, India and educated in St. Stephen's College and JNU Delhi before winning a scholarship to the University of Cambridge, where he was awarded the PhD in History in 1981. His books include *Environment and Ethnicity in India, 1200–1991, Health and Population in South Asia from Earliest Times to the Present,* and *Beyond Caste: Identity and Power in South Asia, Past and Present.*

His most recent book is *History and Collective Memory in South Asia, 1200–2000* (University of Washington Press, 2019). Developing out of the work of Maurice Halbwachs, it is a long-period and comparative study of the frameworks of collective memory. His next work is a study of the political ecology of empires in South Asia from 1400 to 1900.

Acknowledgments

This book owes its origin to the gentle encouragement of Ramya Sreenivasan, who first suggested that I write a comparative trans-Asian study for the AAS. It would not exist without her help and support. Bill Tsutsui and Jon Wilson have helped me concretize the project and answered many questions, both large and small, along the way. When venturing out of my own specialization in South Asia, I have sought the advice of many specialists who took the time to answer numerous queries. I am therefore deeply indebted to Christopher Atwood for sharing his immense knowledge of Mongolia and the Mongols, and to Erdenchuluu Khohchahar for explaining the intricacies of Mongol terminology. Pamela Crossley has answered many rounds of questions about China and the Manchu. Peter Golden took time out of working on a new edition of his classic, *An Introduction to the History of the Turkic Peoples*, to read and comment on an early draft. Alan Mikhail provided an important etymology for an Arabic term. Indrani Chatterjee deepened my understanding of social networks. Johannes Feddema generously offered access to the underlying data for his revision of the Thornthwaite climate map. William Delgado drew a simplified, gray-scale version for this book (Figure 2). Jon Wilson helped create Figure 1 from open access materials. Two anonymous readers read the manuscript closely and offered important suggestions for its improvement. A third reader pointed to significant lacunae—since remedied. Mike Jauchen patiently copyedited the text. Finally, Kirtan Patel read the proofs with an unerring eye for errors. Needless to say, I am of course responsible for any errors, oversimplifications, and overgeneralizations that may be found.

A Note on Transcriptions

I have for the sake of readability sought to eliminate diacritics from this text. Words from Sanskrit, Persian, Hindi, Marathi etc have only been used where essential and transcribed in simple roman script forms. I do not read Mongolian or Chinese and have therefore followed my source in rendering words from these languages. I have however, given Pinyin equivalents in parenthesis for Wade-Giles renderings where necessary. In no case have I changed an author's preferred rendering of her or his name.

CONTENTS

"Did you say pig, or fig?" said the Cat.

"I said pig," replied Alice; "and I wish you wouldn't keep appearing and vanishing so suddenly; you make one quite giddy!"

"All right," said the Cat; and this time it vanished quite slowly, beginning with the end of the tail and ending with the grin, which remained some time after the rest of it had gone.

"Well! I've often seen a cat without a grin," thought Alice; "but a grin without a cat! It's the most curious thing I ever saw in all my life!"

— Lewis Carroll, *Alice's Adventures in Wonderland*

This is a book that tries to do several things simultaneously. It takes a widely employed term — "tribe" — and analyzes the reasons for its current vogue. But it does not confine itself to an academic critique of the popular use of the word: that would be an exercise in futility. It also considers real phenomena that provide "tribe" with its real-world referents. It thus extracts the rational kernel from the pop-cultural shell. Then it grounds the word in its analogues in Asian history and provides them with an intellectual and social genealogy of their own while consistently relating words and things.

The third chapter provides the environmental setting within which the concept has worked. It presents it in the analytic frame of political ecology and shows how tribal formations have adapted to, modified, and reproduced their environment.

The fourth chapter provides a series of short case studies illustrating the theoretical arguments made in the preceding three. In conclusion, the book warns the reader against reifying a social organization: like the Cheshire Cat, the tribe may appear, vanish, and reappear.

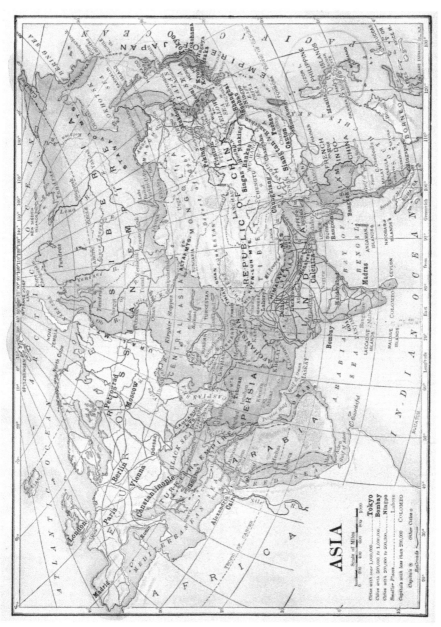

Map 1. Asia physical c.1916. This map illustrates the major geographical divisions of Asia and its placement relative to Africa and Eurasia. Names reflect the cartographer's era. Source: https://commons.wikimedia.org/wiki/File:1916-Asia-political-map.jpg.

INTRODUCTION

"Here, we broke down the five major street style tribes of 2017 so you
can figure out which one you joined—whether you knew it or not."
— Emily Farra, 2017

Tribes are in vogue today.[1] Their primordial existence is routinely invoked
by journalists and academics to explain mass behavior in our own time. This
Anglophone use of "tribe" is of course not new. We shall consider its deeper
history later in this volume. The idea of "tribal feeling" as something primitive,
a throwback to a bygone era, was current and respectable in the great age of
modernization theory that set in after World War II. At that time, "tribalism" was
frequently invoked to explain the political behavior of "not yet modern" (read
non-Western) peoples. In the early 1960s, for example, the well-regarded Clifford
Geertz argued that in "modern" (i.e., Western) societies, calls to "blood and land"
had been transcended by civic sentiments. It was only (he thought) new nation-
states that had seen the reemergence of explosive "tribalism" among other forms
of primordial identity.[2]

For thinkers on both the Right and the Left, modernization, which included the
rise of industrial capitalism, was supposed to dissolve all primordial associations.
Three hundred years ago, John Locke wrote that at the beginning of history, all
the World was America. Three centuries after him, Francis Fukuyama wrote that
at the end of history, all the world would be as America too. History has proven
to be more complex, and back in the USA, "tribalism" is the new word of the
day. A Yale law professor, Amy Chua, has recently published a book claiming that
it was rising tribalism in America that "propelled Trump to the White House."[3]
She then uses "tribal instinct" to explain pretty much every contemporary conflict
known to readers of the *New York Times*'s headlines.[4] The term "tribe" has indeed
acquired an unprecedented prominence in the last two decades. This is even after
social scientists declared it to have little analytic value. A widely read tweet from
a recent president of the United States justified a decision to abandon US allies in

Syria by saying, "it is time for us to get out of these ridiculous endless wars, many of them *tribal*, and bring our soldiers home."[5] It must be evident that a concept of the "tribe" as irredeemably irrational and endlessly violent is implicit in this statement.

The term has thus retained a solid presence in everyday discourse in the early decades of the present century. But we should remember that it is a *sociological label*, a word describing the supposed collective behavior of some persisting social group. It does not describe some innate trait of any group of people. Indeed, in the late twentieth century, professional anthropologists—members of the scholarly discipline that had long used "tribe" to label a type of social organization—were advocating the replacement of "tribe" with "ethnic group." But academic discussion of ethnic groups has then rolled into itself many of the "primordial" traits contained in the popular idea of tribe. The much-cited political scientist Donald Horowitz published *Ethnic Groups in Conflict* in 1985. It analyzed fierce forms of ethnic identity as characteristic of the failure of democracy in non-Western or "Third World" countries. The book assumed, however, that in the enlightened West, a calm civic nationalism had replaced all that. That was also what Geertz had believed.

Horowitz published a new edition of his book in 2000. This one appeared in the aftermath of the Yugoslav civil war, the growing ostracism of and violence against the Roma people, and lesser episodes of ethnic cleansing in the former Soviet bloc. It was impossible to exclude the West from his purview. "Group loyalty" was his euphemism for what the lower-brow Chua has called "tribalism." Horowitz wrote in shock that "group loyalty" had again revealed its murderous aspect "in the heartland of Europe, a half century after Hitler."[6]

Ethnic and national sentiments are now routinely described as "tribal" in order to emphasize their irrational character. This bifurcation is why, disregarding academic critiques of such terminology, popular culture has usually demonized "tribe," even as it has often valorized "ethnic." The latter term is now something interestingly exotic (another word whose connotations have gone from negative to positive). "Ethnic" in the United States is often a neutral or positive characterization. Possessing "ethnic" traits is a selling point for clothes and cuisines alike. The valence of the term has indeed changed from the time when the Church of England's authorized translation of the Bible rendered the Greek word "*ethnos*" as "heathen." But since there is always a psychological need to project societal violence on an exterior "other," the negative, irrational side of "ethnic" loyalty is still described as "tribal."

This is why, despite the rejection of the word by scholars, "tribes" across the world have been in the news in recent years. The tribes of Iraq apparently persisted through Ba'athist single-party rule despite the wealth of the oil boom and the resultant modernization. They were reenergized by the weakening of the Iraqi state following the 1991 Gulf War. They remained important elements of the strategic calculus even under US military occupation. They were significant enough that the United States Congressional Research Service prepared a report on what the author described as Iraq's approximately 150 tribes as of 2007.[7]

The mobilization of the "tribes" was also an important strategy to be employed by US commanders in Iraq and Afghanistan.[8] Leading government functionaries in Iraq, in their moment of supreme crisis, likewise turned to the mobilized "tribes." In 2014, after the failure of the regular army to contain the Islamic State, a press release by the official Iraqi news agency quoted the defense minister who pinned his hopes on a new brigade of 2,000 volunteers. This brigade was drawn from the recognized social organizations whose Arabic names were rendered in the press release as "clans" and "tribes." "It was agreed to form / the elite brigade / [which] consists of 25 clans includes / 2000 / fighters from the sons of those tribes."[9] Similarly, the BBC published an analytic report on politics in oil-rich Libya in 2011 that took the superiority of tribal cohesion over military discipline for granted. The report stated:

> tribal rivalries are evident within the armed forces, where Mr Gaddafi's own tribe, the Qadhadfa, are pitted against Magariha . . . which are close to the Warfalla tribe, said to number one million people. In turn, the Warfalla are close to the Al-Zintan.[10]

Such terminology was not confined to disturbed regions and collapsing states. Amnesty International described how the political and judicial authority of what it described as "tribal" assemblies and chieftains continued to exist in the much more stable sociopolitical setting of central Pakistan.[11]

"Tribe" is, therefore, clearly "good to think" (to borrow a phrase from Levi-Strauss). It is a term that repeatedly surges up into popular media discourse to describe certain kinds of sociopolitical organization and collective behavior. It is, therefore, necessary to think about it too. This book will seek to induce the reader to think about this common noun and its historical denotations in order to better understand its use and abuse in the present. My goal is to extract the rational kernel from a loosely used term while also demonstrating the mutability of all social organization over time.

But may it not be argued that "tribe" has become so diffuse as to have lost all specific content? Let me reiterate: "tribe" is a term used to label certain communities of people, their consciousness, and their way of life. It does not describe some palpable entity, like the liver or Achilles tendon. The label has been used differently in various places and times. It has a history, and this book will unpack some of that history.

I think it is nonetheless unwise—indeed impractical—to completely reject the word: first, because the reader will assuredly encounter it in the global public square, and second, because it now has equivalents in several Asian languages. Indeed, across the former British Empire in South Asia and elsewhere, the term is a widely understood loanword. It is used in many settings, whether when opposing dam projects or selling jewelry, artwork, and fabrics. It is also a legal and administrative term. The government of Thailand runs special development projects, access to which depends on applicants' securing official identification as a "Thai Hill Tribe."[12] The republic of India uses the term to define over 100 million people who are entitled to special rights and protections. As the communities are listed in a special "Schedule" within the Constitution of India, they are officially described as "Scheduled Tribes." The term is used to label institutes and organizations that focus their activities around these communities. In Pakistan, a politically important region was (until recently) officially known as the Federally Administered Tribal Area. In colonial times, the area was subject to a different legal regime, one that allowed for collective punishment. That legal regime had its origins in the colonial belief that tribes automatically protected their own members. It followed that the only way to persuade malefactors to surrender was to coerce the community to which they belonged by ravaging its fields and villages.[13]

Historical Patterns of Kingless "Tribal" Organization

Media popularity and administrative use do not, of course, justify the adoption of a term. But I argue that the word "tribe" is useful to maintain the distinction between the tightly structured domains governed by Emperors, Kings, Dear Leaders, Stable Geniuses, and such, and the looser patterns of decentralized polities, systems without a single, powerful head. (Social anthropologists call the *most* decentralized of these "acephalous," or literally "headless," political systems.) Acephalous communities tolerated no autocrats who might do as they pleased. They would only need leadership in particular settings and from time to time. So they might be governed by war chiefs chosen for an emergency period or by colleges of priests. In more organized settings, certain aristocratic lineages might possess a recognized right to provide leaders when needed. But leadership roles were temporary.

The Russian scholars Bondarenko, Grinin, and Korotayev recently edited an important volume on the appearance and disappearance of states in human history. Their introduction presented the various forms of authority that have characterized complex human societies after the rise of agriculture (or "the domestication of plants and animals"). Monarchies by definition are characterized by a single powerful ruler. But it was also possible for states to be "heterarchies," to have different authorities controlling different aspects of collective life. Heterarchic societies possess several governors or multiple power centers. Crosscutting hierarchies, the authors argued, ensured that no one was inferior or superior in all of them. Bondarenko, Grinin, and Korotayev rejected simple evolutionary models that claimed that there had to be an inevitable movement from the emergence of social inequality to a single hierarchical ordering of it. They showed that this progression is not as inevitable as many social scientists have believed. There is instead a continuum of variation through time. Messianic and charismatic leaders may arise and overcome faction and division, leading people in an effort to create or attain paradise. Some chiefs and leaders might go on to build great empires riven by inequality and hierarchy. At other times, social groups small and large might be left to their own devices of self-government and mutual aid. In that setting, collective decisions were infrequent and taken by councils of elders or the "white beards," the few old men to be found in any small settlement.

Political anthropologists, therefore, now see many entities as occupying the vast range of community organizations above the truly acephalous. The latter are conceived as simple bands of ten or twenty persons, characteristic of hunting and gathering communities. These were once the only form of human organization but are now practically extinct. At the other extreme are centralized, imperial bureaucratic states ruled by divine rulers.[14] Between these two extremes are intermediate organizations, both small and large, that may be seen as durable forms of collective life. They may, like bricks, be cemented into monumental ziggurats of imperial greatness but also left strewn across the land whenever such a Tower of Babel collapses.

What I term "tribal organization" may then be considered a station or location along the range from a simple band—perhaps five or six nomad tents or bamboo shelters of shifting cultivators—up to thousands of such clusters merged into a complex confederation. At each level of complexity, alternative forms of organization could be found. In the Middle East, with its extensive records, it is possible to show that many tribes arose out of the political disintegration of the more centralized chiefdoms "that had preceded them in time."[15] Equally, of course, conquest states could emerge out of looser entities, especially if there were wealthy but vulnerable societies in the vicinity. Conquering tribes might grow into states, devolve into bands, or dissolve untraceably into larger entities, especially into the more successful of the modern nation-states. We may think of such organizations as existing along a continuum, from simple bands of pastoralists, to swidden (pejoratively called 'slash and burn') farmers and hunters, and up to empires like the thirteenth-century Mongols. There is thus a spectrum of organization. At the lowest, or "coolest," its heat signature is invisible to the human eye. Then, as its temperature rises, radiation may be felt as warmth. At yet higher temperatures, a red, and then a white-hot glow, appears to our gaze. Like molten iron, a messianic movement or tribal invasion flows in a shower of blinding sparks—and then perhaps everything cools once more. The hot stage is analogous to the tribal empire that melts and reshapes previous bands into new formations that then cool down into residual simpler entities, now perhaps far distant from their ancestral homes.[16]

The tribe would thus commonly appear as an adaptive mechanism in phases of state weakness or failure. Even though Mesopotamia was historically the birthplace of kingdoms and empires, yet tribal organization has persisted there, even if specific tribes have repeatedly dissolved and vanished. The modernizing Ottoman state briefly asserted itself in the early twentieth century before collapsing at the end of World War I. The new British occupiers restored power to pliable tribal sheikhs in order to stabilize their own rule.[17] The destruction of the modern Libyan state by NATO intervention only spurred a visible revival of tribal warlords that persists to this day.[18] Tribes might appear also as defensive and offensive leagues on the periphery of states, in ungoverned or weakly governed areas, and then move on to overwhelm states.[19]

I therefore reject the tendency to attribute timeless, stable traits to peoples who, at some periods in history, were organized in "tribes," or recognizable analogues of that term, across Asia. I argue instead that tribalism is a recurring political phenomenon in history, not a long-past phase of human social evolution. As Fredrik Barth wrote, the "Middle East is the homeland of states and empires; it has known centralized political systems far longer than any other region of the world. . . . The tribal peoples that are found in the region do not retain their tribal institutions through ignorance, but as a stable and successful adaptation to the natural and social environment in which they find themselves."[20]

The Social Psychology of Tribal Peoples

In the 1950s, Karl Wittfogel remarked that in early states, the power of the few depended on the submission of the many. That submission was psychically costly for early, relatively egalitarian peoples, who were prepared to endure lean years and even long periods of famine to avoid subjugation. This, he wrote, demonstrates "the immense attraction of nonmaterial values, when increased material security can be attained only at the price of political, economic, and cultural submission."[21] It is worth visualizing what "submission" meant in performance. Let me give a striking example of rituals of abasement in hierarchical societies, as described by the historian S. D. Goitein, who witnessed it. A newly arrived immigrant Jew from Yemen came up to another Yemeni who had long been settled in the new republic of Israel and who worked as an attendant in the transit camp. The newcomer "in a fraction of a second threw himself down on the ground before the attendant, kissing his feet and embracing his legs, while making some trivial request. The mere physical aspect was quite remarkable. Throwing oneself down on the ground with such force without getting hurt showed that the man must have long practice in such matters."[22] The cultivated, German-born Goitein was repelled by the sight. We can only imagine what free peasants or herdsmen would have thought if they had been required to routinely perform such acts of ritual abasement.

The recoil from such daily humiliation might be why socially open societies have long been seen as being characterized by individual behaviors that are different from those of hierarchical ones. An egalitarian social situation would therefore manifest itself in personal comportment, lifeways, customs, and values. Imperial intellectuals generally viewed kingless tribes and barbarian bands with disdain and fear. Therefore, Chinese strategists said that the peoples bordering the pastoral lands of Inner Asia were "proud and stubborn, high-spirited and fond of feats of daring and evil."[23]

The conscious cultivation of a ferocious affect would be a social asset during interactions *across* ethnic boundaries but fissiparous *within* the group. We may take the much-studied Yusufzai of western Pakistan and eastern Afghanistan as an example. Sections of the tribe exacted tolls on important passes: a threatening appearance and a corresponding readiness for violence were needed in such transactions. They also formed a landlord minority in the fertile Swat Valley, where they domineered over the rest of the population. A ferocious bearing, then, was a marker of an elite status that was cross-culturally comprehensible as a lordly trait. Consequently, it was effective in deeply stratified societies such as the Swat Valley and even more so in the interior of the Indian subcontinent, but less so in Afghanistan itself.[24] Elphinstone wrote in 1815:

> The manners of the Afghauns are frank and open. Though manly and independent, they are entirely free from that affectation of military pride and ferocity which is so conspicuous in their descendants, the Pitans [Pathans] of India. When their address is bad, it is rustic, but never fierce or insolent; the Indian Pitans seem to have copied the peculiar manners of the Eusofzyes, to whom a haughty and arrogant carriage is natural.[25]

Other sources confirm this trait. The experienced John Malcolm, for example, noted that the "Patans from Hindustan" [North India] and the Purbia [eastern Indian] Brahmans who enlisted in infantry units were marked by both a rudeness of manners and a turbulence of character. They were equally hated and feared by the inhabitants of Central India.[26] A century later, an experienced rural official in Western India described how "Rohila," Kabuli, and Pathan moneylenders could extort their demands by intimidation, without having to go through the courts. They were tall, rubicund, robust, and ferocious, and their debtors feared them too much to resist their demands. They were sometimes hired to collect debts, in which case two or three of them would dress like Indian army soldiers and molest and harass debtor households in illegal ways.[27]

Psychological categorization through habitat and temperament was common beyond South Asia too. I begin with material in Fiskesjö's survey of Chinese classifications of outsiders ("barbarians"). He argues that the binary division translated by the binary of "Raw" and "Cooked" is still valid, but it especially applies to the assimilable lands and people to the south and east. Of the (southern) Li, one text wrote:

> Raw Li, though simple and straightforward, are brutish and aggressive. They do not accept impositions or affronts, but still, they are not, after all, an affliction on our people. But the Cooked Li, for the most part, are faithless folk from Hu-Guang, and Fujian: they are sly, cruel, misfortune-bringing rascals.[28]

It is, however, evident that the internal organization of such groups was not considered in that passage, only their conduct and temperament as viewed by the exterior elite. Therefore, as Peter Golden has pointed out, no civilized intellectual suggested that "the harsh warrior ethos of 'Barbarian' society was in no small measure, a response to the threats, encroachments and attempts at political manipulation coming from the settled world."[29] It is historically evident, however, that the said encroachments were more successful in some places than others.

The Political Ecology of Kingless Societies

The great Arab thinker, Ibn Khaldun (1332–1406), considered the ensemble of lifeways and attitudes that shaped rural communities in contrast to those of sedentary urban people. Communities, he reasoned, adjusted to their predominant mode of production. People in the simplest communities resembled each other. This arose from their uniform conditions of life. As a consequence, they possessed a mutual solidarity (*asabiyya*). They needed to rely on each other as they had no walls or mercenaries to guard them. Rural and nomadic people were thus endowed with a certain ferocious solidarity that made them militarily formidable. They were good soldiers because of their "desert qualities, desert toughness, and desert savagery."[30]

Khaldun perceived an environmental gradient that shaped character. Rural people were hardier and more self-reliant than townspeople. But there was a gradient even outside the cities. Farmers were tied to their fields, and keepers of sheep and cattle could not venture where their animals could not subsist. Of all the nomadic peoples, therefore, it was camel nomads (whom he often referred to simply as "Arabs") who traveled most deeply into the true deserts. This was partly because their animals needed this habitat and its salty water. But they also fled there to escape punishment for their depredations in settled areas. As Khaldun noted, "As a result, they are the most savage human beings that exist. Compared with sedentary people, they are on a level with wild, untamable (animals) and dumb beasts of prey."[31] The great Arab scholar was born in North Africa, but his analysis, if we remove his value judgments, applies across Eurasia. Indeed, his report of the speech he made to the Turkic conqueror Timur, in 1401, presents the transcontinental ambit of his thought. Ibn Khaldun reports that he said, "Power is at its greatest extent among mainly tribal peoples, those whose lives are governed by tribal solidarity. Men of science are agreed that the two most tribal peoples on earth are the Turks and the Arabs."[32]

Ibn Khaldun also saw tribal conquests as cyclical: urban, affluent polities grew effete and were renewed by tribal conquests. But then the conquerors themselves succumbed to the effete ways of civilization. Once they lost their martial qualities, the cycle began anew. It would follow, then, that the persistence of tribal organization was a permanent aspect of the overall social order. Thus, Khaldun's political ecology linked temperament, habitat, and solidarity into a cyclical model of history.

Khaldun's translator, the historian Franz Rosenthal, argued that the former believed this powerful solidarity could even exist among folk "not related to each other by blood ties but by long and close contact as members of a group."[33] Such contact naturally existed among the small communities of the unprotected countryside. The idea that a tribal community could be shaped by virtue of its environment rather than by simple "ties of blood" anticipated much later anthropological thought. Khaldun thus pioneered the linking of environment and lifeway with social organization in a way that clearly inspired the twentieth-century concept of "habitus" developed by Pierre Bourdieu.[34]

As we saw, however, Khaldun, a townsman, statesman, and scholar, shared the general contempt for savage nomads characteristic of the civilized world. But he also knew them well, having spent years among them and having more than once mobilized tribesmen to install and overthrow sultans in several North African cities. His appreciation of their strengths was based on deep personal experience.[35] Many West Asian rulers, like Timur, whom Khaldun admired and flattered, were known to be of recent steppe nomad origin. The environment of Inner Asia only allowed stable tillage in oasis islets in the arid sea of sand or savanna.

The habitat of Southwest Asia was less restrictive, but still confined arable farming to limited areas—mountain slopes, valleys, or around costly irrigation sources. It meant that Inner Asian tribal peoples maintained a steady presence in the region. In the eighteenth and nineteenth centuries, nomads comprised from a quarter to a half of the population of Iran. A. K. S. Lambton wrote that until the twentieth century, all "except the strongest governments have delegated responsibility in the tribal areas to the tribal chiefs." Many chiefs also served as generals, and some, like Nadir Shah Afshar, refounded a Persian kingdom after an earlier tribal attack had destroyed the previous dynasty.[36] Habitats in South Asia on the other hand, could vary over smaller areas and shorter periods of time. This, as I argue in chapter 3, produced the greater variability of the Indian subcontinent, the instability of its political systems and the resulting mobile landscape. If the classic Inner Asian transition was from nomad chief to kingly conqueror, the South Asian one was from woodland raider to warden of the borderlands to lordly feudatory. As there were many such feudatory roles, it is likely that the transition was made more often than elsewhere in Asia. Some Indian legends and mythic texts reflect this situation: the many woodlands served as bases and refuges for rulers in waiting.[37]

The Plan of This Work

Chapter 1 will explore the conceptualization of tribe-like entities as an analytic category in different Asian civilizations. It is, however, an inescapable fact that for the past two centuries, the world has been dominated by Western powers. The analytic categories produced from their metropolitan academic establishments were deployed worldwide: they formed the basis of the projects of modernization and revival urgently sought by the Asian intelligentsia of the nineteenth and twentieth century. Chapter 2 has been prefigured in the opening paragraph of this introduction but will offer a deeper exploration, considering how the modern English word "tribe" and associated concepts were developed even as that term was deployed in Asia. It will therefore review the many ways in which it has been applied through centuries down to the present.

Deserts, extensive pastures, and forests have often been seen in both Asia and Europe as the habitat that generated and sheltered tribes. Chapter 3 will consequently present the varying "political ecology" of tribal formations across Asia. Chapter 4, the book's longest chapter, offers case studies of the historical trajectories of what are today accepted as tribes across Asia, from the Bosporus east to the Sea of Japan, and from the Arctic Circle south to the Indian Ocean. It gives the reader a more concrete understanding of the many ways these entities were born and the metamorphoses they have undergone to the present.

Finally, the reader will have observed that I have narrowed my focus from the global connotations of the term 'tribe' to its Asian limits (expansively understood). This restriction is needed to limit the work to a manageable size and also to conform to the Asia Shorts series.

1

ASIAN IDEAS OF "TRIBE"

"Obtaining the support of a tribal force is the best [kind of armed support]..."
  — *Arthashastra* (11.1.1)

Perspectives: From Within, from Above, and from Below

During the high era of Western imperial dominance that ended with World War II, Euro-American analysts automatically assumed that the analytic terms they employed were intellectually superior to the indigenous ones used by the peoples they studied. A consideration of the history of that Western set of categories appears in the next chapter. But Asians had reflected on their own social organization long before Western sociologists appeared on the scene. "Social organization" is an academic term that selectively summarizes many social daily interactions— interactions so routine as to be internalized and expected of self and others. Early Asian intellectuals analyzed and evaluated these. We shall now consider their variations across the great regions of historical Asia. 'Tribe' is not a word from any Asian language. So can we legitimately use it?

Peter Golden, a major historian of Inner Asia, recently argued that regardless of social scientific critiques, the peoples of Eurasia had terms equivalent to "tribe" and its various subbranches and clans, "which are found in their own documents and in the documents of their contemporaries. These terms had meaning for them, even if they may seem somewhat imprecise to modern observers."[1] This chapter will explore these historically changing uses of analogous terms by Asians before the recasting of their social thought by Western dominance. Furthermore, as we embark on a consideration of names and concepts, I should point out that the appearance of a name normally follows the formation of the social phenomenon it labels. Such phenomena would be "institutionally fully present before anyone fumbled for a word by which to designate them."[2] But I will not assume there was any uniform Asian or indigenous point of view. As Pieke wrote in a study of modern Chinese anthropological thought, "[c]ultures are fields of discursive contention between many different native viewpoints."[3] One should therefore avoid imposing a single unchanging Asian viewpoint just as one should avoid using a similarly monolithic Western one.

In the 1930s and 1940s, Western anthropologists began to more actively seek indigenous or "native models" of social organization rather than analyze all societies with imported categories. The diversity of indigenous viewpoints soon became evident. Thus, Edmund Leach sought to comprehend the wide array of political organization across the multilingual, ecologically diverse Kachin Hills region of northern Burma (now Myanmar). He found "two polar types" known regionally as *gumlao* and *gumsa*. The first was a "'democratic' species of organization" in which the political entity was a single village without marked class differences; the second was an "'aristocratic' species of organization," where a larger territory was subordinate to a prince of aristocratic lineage. He also elicited each community's opinion of the other. Leach found that *gumsa* communities described the *gumlao* as commoner serfs who had revolted against their lawful masters; *gumlao* regarded *gumsa* as tyrants and snobs.[4]

What of the longer historical epoch before Western records, however? Durable literary artifacts that survive for later historians are typically created by state-patronized intellectuals. They therefore only exist in hierarchical settings. Surviving realistic texts of premodern political theory in Asia or Europe were typically a product of the intelligentsia affiliated with emergent states. Only kingdoms and empires needed and sustained such specialists, men who created durable records. Other points of view are, of course, sometimes represented in the evidence, especially where formerly oral tradition and myth have crystallized into written form. But they are inevitably refracted through the gaze of the intelligentsia and its patrons. Even works such as the *Secret History of the Mongols*, which preserved early traditions of the Borjigid line from which Chinggis Khan emerged, were written some decades after the establishment of his empire, though the exact Year of the Rat when it was completed is uncertain.[5] The simple nomad camp is already depicted as a lifeway doomed to perish. The early hero Bodonchar is represented as equating egalitarianism with weakness.

> "These people who are staying on the Tunggelik rivulet make no distinction between great and small, bad and good, high and mean: they are all equal. *They are a people easy to take.* Let us attack them!" His elder

brother said: "Very well. If this is so, as soon as we reach home we will consult with our brothers and we will attack those people."[6]

The attack succeeded, and the disorganized people were robbed and subjugated. The subtext is clearly imperial Chinggisid: subordination gave strength. Those who had rejected it in favor of autonomy and equality would end up as captives and subjects. But considered specifically, the episode only represented the value of simple tribal leadership. Even the victors, Bodonchar and his brothers, were organized through no more than the genealogical subordination of younger to older, accompanied by fraternal consultation, solidarity, and unified military action.

Tribespeople themselves often saw an egalitarian boldness as an essential feature of their identity. The Pathan or "native model" of being Pathan, Barth wrote, emphasized "male autonomy and egality [sic], self-expression and aggressiveness." These qualities were manifested and judged in three related domains: hospitality, which was the honorable use of wealth; tribal councils, which were the situations in which a man presented himself in the honorable conduct of public affairs; and domestic seclusion, which was honor expressed in the domestic setting. The anthropologist Akbar S. Ahmed, while often critical of Barth, confirmed the characterization of Pashtun identity in these terms. Speakers of the ethnic language who did not manifest these values in everyday conduct were "speaking, but not doing Pashto." Barth wrote that Pathans from the socially homogenous southern tribes found the landlord-dominated structure of the Swat Valley so repugnant that they declared the people there were "no longer Pathan." Akbar Ahmed, who conducted his fieldwork several decades after Barth, also agreed that the distinction was so intense that Pathan communities would reject those who lived in stratified communities as no longer "doing Pashto."[7]

Evidence for plebeian understanding of their own special organization is, therefore, not altogether lacking. The rejection of hierarchy and a corresponding aggressive desire for autonomy was not an idea imposed upon these peoples by outside observers like Barth or Ibn Khaldun. It was valued within many of these communities. Elphinstone, then a young British officer on a diplomatic mission, interviewed many Afghans in 1809–1810, at a time when their lands lay far beyond the edge of the British Empire in India. He wrote the first historical ethnology of this people. He reported that ordinary men prided themselves on their independence, and, when he urged an old man as to the benefits of submission to a sovereign, the latter replied with great warmth and indignation. The indignant harangue ended with a denunciation of arbitrary power: "We are content with discord, we are content with alarms, we are content with blood, but we will never be content with a master." Several of Elphinstone's informants also recited a popular verse summarizing the characteristics of a well-ordered country. It should be stateless—

or, at any rate, one where "no one, but no one" (*kasi, hich kasi*) had the authority to inquire into another man's doings. He was also told that Pashto-speaking Afghans looked down on Dari-speaking townspeople, terming them Deggaun or Dehkaun (originally *dehqan*, village lord, later meaning peasant). Uzbegs similarly referred to urban folk as "Serds or Serts", originally meaning trader, townsman, or caravan leader. Both were terms of contempt, reflecting the perception that such people were subject to others.[8] All tribal subgroups were named after an ancestor, and these again were supposed to originate from a common ancestor, so as a twentieth century anthropologist observed, "the tribal system looks exactly like a family genealogy."[9]

Other peoples valued their autonomy too. Around 1811, a large hilltop encampment of insurgent Bhil tribals that had been plundering villages in Central India was approached by a royal emissary. He advised them to submit to his master. They retorted, "we are kings of the forest, our ways are different, do you not worry your head with them."[10] A similar assertion of dominance is found in the preferred ethnonym "Girasia" among Koli and Bhil tribals in Western India. "Giras "was a tribute paid by villages and traders for protection, or at any rate, immunity from plunder. Possessing a share in it was an assertion of at least local dominance, of a sharing in the attributes of suzerainty.[11] Thus, perception and the self-presentation of temperament, behavior, and organization flowed into each other. Entire Bhil communities used Girasia as a collective or tribal name. An aspiration to dominance is embedded in that adoption.

Historically speaking, we know that radical counter-visions that critiqued emerging kingly states were current too. But it is mainly their religious and mythic expression that has entered the scribal record. In the Hebrew tradition, the wise judge Samuel was inspired to warn the people of Israel against having a king. The king would be a man who would turn their sons and daughters into his servants, would seize their best lands and give them to his own men, and oppress them in various ways.[12] In South Asia, Gautama, the founder of Buddhism, was born in a republican community that was destroyed by the rising kingdom of Magadha two generations after the Buddha's death. The religious order he founded is known as the Sangha, a word also used in some early texts for what we would call "tribe." The Buddhist idea that there had once been an age of natural simplicity and abundance, before covetousness spawned private property and made kingship necessary, is an example of a mythic counter-discourse. Initially, no authority was needed, but then the decay of morals led people to elect kings to check theft and misconduct. In return, rulers were to receive a share of the grain produced. One Buddhist Sutta text sought to minimize the power of kings and remind them that they should please the people (and not oppress them). It declared:

"The People's Choice" is the meaning of Maha-Sammata, which is the first regular title to be introduced. "Lord Of The Fields" is the meaning of Khattiya, the second such title. And "He Gladdens Others With Dhamma" is the meaning of Raja, the third title to be introduced.[13]

The Buddhist historical tradition thus took a favorable view of kingless states and sought to minimize legitimate kingly authority wherever it became absolutely necessary. Various discourses attributed to the Buddha enunciated norms such as mutual trust and collective counsel, to which republican communities should adhere if they wished to preserve their independent power.[14] The author or authors whether Biblical or Buddhist, clearly valorized a kingless political order which was nonetheless autonomous and self-governed. More complex theories and descriptions came from kingly and imperial settings. These varied across Asia and so must be considered regionally.

Inner East Asia: The Emergence of a Tribe-State Frontier

I will begin in the east, where the core civilization of the region emerged in today's north-central China. Chinese literati associated with early kingdoms began to make a fundamental distinction between their own Middle Kingdom and foreign peoples who lived in the four directions around it. Successive empires sought to create "hard" administrative boundaries. They also sought to know and subjugate peoples within the boundary by requiring household registration. This became a consistent imperial policy as warring kingdoms were crushed into a universal empire. Once registered and enumerated, individuals and families were liable to regulation and taxation by the state.[15]

Those physically within the claimed imperial boundaries could be classified into three categories: unassimilated, partly assimilated, and entirely integrated. The last of these classes would be subordinated and internally stratified peoples. Fiskesjö argues that this classificatory gradient marked the distinction between Chinese terms often translated as the "Raw" and the "Cooked." He adds that "[o]ther translations ('unadministered/administered,' 'uncivilised/civilized,' etc.) seem elaborate but are actually less accurate. For application to China's barbarians, 'Raw/Cooked' definitely remains the best translation (and probably also remains more suitable for the contemporary Chinese usage, since it renders these metaphors more transparent)." Fiskesjö argues, furthermore, that those whom it was impossible to "cook", i.e., subordinate into conformity—such as the northern pastoralists who lived in lands impossible for sustained farming—had to be excluded from the classification. That exclusion was marked upon the face of the earth by great walls built to keep them out.[16] Their political formations were not amenable to imperial rule. The earliest agrarian kingdoms of the emergent Chinese civilization made enormous efforts to demarcate and exclude the nomads of the north and west. But many of these walls cut off highly productive parts of pastoral habitat, such as the Ordos region of the Yellow River Valley. This was one of the intermediate zones identified by Khazanov, zones where deep agricultural traditions lived in tension with nomad pastoralism.[17]

The mixed farmers and pastoralists of the intermediate area were not, at this time, formidable antagonists. Di Cosmo observes that early North Chinese states were able to contain and defeat the nomads without much difficulty. General Meng Tien (Meng Dian) drove them out of the Ordos altogether. The loss of territory long used as pasture would have precipitated a subsistence crisis. That crisis, Di Cosmo argues, created the opportunity for new, more centralized leadership to replace the older elite. This, then, was a result of Chinese state incursions into nomad lands. These aggressions forced the nomads to mobilize and create additional levels of hierarchy, with a supreme charismatic leader at the top.[18]

Descriptions in Chinese sources indicate that the nomad pastoralists ("all who draw the bow") encountered by emerging Chinese states had already organized themselves into hereditary status groups. The Hsiung-nu (Xiong-nu) had twenty-four, the Turks twenty-eight. The chiefs of each were reported to appoint subordinate chiefs over thousands, hundreds, and tens of households. The upper-level groups of thousands and hundreds are clearly equivalent to what we would consider tribes. In times of consolidated empire, some tribes became superior to others. Such processes helped create the early nomad consolidation that became known as the Hsiung-nu (Xiong-nu) Empire. Its name illustrative of the power of sedentary states and their literati to shape discourse. "Hsiung-nu (Xiong-nu)" was a Chinese coinage and the characters used had the meaning "fierce slave."[19]

The Han Empire was frequently forced to accept humiliating terms at the hands of "fierce slaves," however, before it reorganized its military by borrowing from steppe tactics. Its armies were then able to break up and subdue the Xiong-nu. At that point, the latter seem to have disintegrated from an imperial confederation into simpler "tribal" units under individual chiefs. Yü writes that the groups submitting to the Han were led by many distinct chiefs—as many as seventy in one instance. In another example, fifty-eight different groups aggregating 200,000 people submitted. That would be an average of less than 4,000 persons each—perhaps 800 tents. Yet since each negotiated terms of surrender, it must be obvious that each of these groups possessed some internal coherence of their own. That coherence was then recognized by Han literati officials who counted the units as being such.[20] Over 1,200 years later, following the disintegration of the Mongol (Yuan) Empire after 1360, the Ordos region of North China was once again populated by nomad peoples who must be characterized as "tribes." A Chinese official reported to the Ming emperor around 1570 that tens of thousands of people lived there, but they were divided into forty-two branches, each of which claimed primacy. Each had only a few thousand members, sometimes only one to two thousand.[21] Average community size therefore had not changed much over this great span of time. Whatever the names used for them, these were obviously small tribal societies led by individual chiefs. The cycle of disintegration and reintegration was a recurring one on the Inner Asian frontier.

Formal consideration of nomad pastoral social organization by Chinese literati came after Ch'in (Qin) and Han times. This may have been influenced by the reality of nomads—first the Khitan (Liao dynasty) and then the Jurchen (Jin dynasty)—building sizable kingdoms in what were recognizably parts of former Han China itself. The Jurchen even conquered all North China and drove the Song dynasty into the south. Their simple, or "tribal," organization was noted by Chinese observers. Important affairs, a Song report said, were concerted by clan leaders who gathered in open country and traced sketches in the ground during their debate. Those of lower status spoke first. Rulers and common Jurchen folk also ate and drank together in what was clearly a display of solidarity. Furthermore, when "everyone was drunk, all people [including the ruler] would dance together." Such informality was shocking to Chinese literati. But when the defeat of the Liao made newly emerged Jurchen kings into overlords over a large Chinese population and many cities, they shaped a dual administration: one for the conquering tribe and one for their Chinese subjects. The conquerors were grouped into notional units of one thousand, with an appointed or recognized chief (*bojilie*) over each. In the first twenty years of the conquest, Khitan and Chinese were also appointed to command these followings. The units could then be deployed as necessary. The king was himself "supreme chief" (*du bojilie*). In effect, then, groups of nomad warriors under old or new chiefs were molded into ethnic garrisons by the conquest state. Hang points out that this prefigured the famous Manchu military banner system created by the Qing dynasty.[22] It may not be coincidental that it was in this post-Tang era, one when Chinese literati had to adapt to serving nomad conquerors, that a new Chinese character combination naming coresidential militias under their own chiefs appeared.

I draw here on the work of Christopher Atwood, who has however, criticized English translators' overuse of "tribe" to translate Chinese ethnonyms, especially the character combination *buluo*. Atwood defined tribe as "kin-based rather than territory-based, segmentary rather than functionally organized, corporate rather than individual in its property relations, and relatively unstratified by wealth." He agreed *buluo* was similar to tribe only in one sense: it was used solely for social divisions within polities that were "seen as less civilized and unequal to the center (in this case, China)." He continued however, that the connotations of *buluo* are quite different from those of "tribe" in Western anthropological literature. Atwood, therefore, protested the frequent insertion of the word "tribe" in translations of Chinese texts where the original only had used merely a specific ethnic name. He added that the arbitrariness of these insertions of "tribes" into English translations "is accentuated by the fact that the term 'tribe' is not inserted into the translation of the chapters on the oasis people of Central Asia or the proto-Korean kingdom of Chaoxian ...—again without any basis in a distinction in the Chinese original."

The combination of the characters, *bu* and *luo* he continues, indicated "the fusion of military leadership with civil leadership. Thus the peacetime village was the wartime band; one man was both peacetime judge and wartime commander." It was only about 1000 CE, Atwood continued, that an additional character combination appeared: *buzu*. In an article analyzing the thought of Ouyang Xiu, a mid-eleventh-century Chinese scholar, Atwood described Ouyang's consistent use of the term *buzu*, a binome combining *bu*, "a group of people following one leader," and *zu*, a "descent group" or "clan." This might seem to indicate that Ouyang believed that corporate kin groups as political units "were particularly characteristic of the barbarians." This combined the character for "descent group" with that for "following" to create a term also often rendered into English as "tribe." But Ouyang's text "carefully distinguishes cases where the residence groups were based on kinship and when they were not, although what exactly the priority of the residence group or the descent group meant in any particular case is not explicitly defined."

Thus, the entity described was clearly very similar to "the nineteenth-twentieth century anthropological meaning of tribe or clan as a unit held together by kin or quasi-kin ties." I would point out that even if it had not occurred any earlier, at least by the eleventh century Chinese literati had recognized and named the socio-political organization that had violently intruded upon the Middle Kingdom.[23]

I would also argue that the nomenclatural problem results from what Alec Nove, a historian of the USSR, famously described as a comparison of "model" with "muddle", of an idealized capitalism or communism with its messy, real world antagonist. The textbook tribe may not have borne much resemblance to the semantic reading of *buluo*. But the classic model of the kin-based segmentary tribe invoked by Atwood was developed by Evans-Pritchard for the Nuer peoples of the Sudan around 1940. Even at the time, other anthropologists of Africa were pointing out that it did not conform to reality on the ground. Audrey Richards, in her review of Evans-Pritchard's book, wrote that "the lack of permanence of particular lineages or 'segments'; the infinite variety there is in their composition, their liability to change owing to historic factors, the strength of individual personalities and similar determinants" meant that his elegant model did not fit the messy reality of East Africa.[24] To recapitulate therefore: Atwood argues that earlier character combinations routinely glossed as "tribe" in English translations of early Chinese histories did not in fact refer to anything like the closed descent group he found defined as "tribe" in anthropological literature. He continues that it was only after the Tang era that "barbarian" societies were described as being organized in kin groups.

This is not surprising. The name of a societal structure will probably not appear until long after the structure itself is known. This is doubly the case if it is the name of a structural element in an alien or barbarian society. Furthermore, the genealogically deep ancestral descent group was viewed as a civilized Chinese institution: admitting that exterior groups also possessed it might admit a parity of status between them and the literati of the Middle Kingdom. It may be that it was the avoidance of this dangerous admission that caused Ouyang to skeptically scrutinize the possibility of the nomads having authentic genealogies like his own. He then argued that nomads could not have a stable, genealogically sound, political and social order. This was because they did not possess distinct written records and, therefore, could not have durable and authentic descent groups as represented (in his view) by Chinese lineages. Atwood has translated Ouyang's discussion of the instability of genealogy resulting from the nomads' lack of family names and records.

> As the barbarians make their dwelling place and eat and drink, they follow the water and grass and migrate according to the heat and cold. They have leaders and tribal names but are without any lasting descent groups (*shizu*) or distinct written records, so when it comes to the weak and the strong consuming each other with their twanging bows and poisoned arrows and the varying sizes of their countries and the instability of the rise and fall, how could there be adequate basis to investigate any of this?[25]

This leaves us with a paradox. Ouyang thought "tribes" (*buzu*) were based on kin relationships, but that the truth of these relationships could never be solidly established. Nomadic life was inherently unstable, and the absence of written records prevented real genealogical study. Implicitly, he (not unsurprisingly) assumed that Chinese genealogies were historical, but barbarian ones were fanciful. We need not adopt this distinction. Historically fictive relationships can still be socially real and effective.

The single ancestor from whom many tribes—or entire peoples, like the Afghans—traced their descent was often clearly fictitious. Elphinstone said as much two centuries ago. When discussing the supposed descent of all Afghans from one Qais, who went to Mecca and converted to Islam in the seventh century CE, Elphinstone pointed to some inconsistencies when compared with the Arab historians and other sources. He shrewdly discerned that this did not matter. Accepted genealogies were, in his view, the functional frame for Afghan political organization. We may conclude that the kin-group is relevant as a political, social, and property-holding unit, but it is no firmer in its boundaries than the tribe. Chinese analysts like Ouyang Xiu seem to have recognized this malleability even if they thought Chinese genealogies were indeed stable and authentic.

As long as a tribe (say the Yusufzai of Afghanistan) acts in solidarity, the historical reality of the ancestral Yusuf is irrelevant. The lack of records would in fact facilitate the adjustment of genealogies to current sociopolitical needs. In what I term "tribally organized societies," lines of tribal loyalty and affiliation supplied the place of baron and king in European feudalism. The instability of "the rise and fall" could be accommodated only by thinly documented genealogies. Deletions and insertions could be made seamlessly. Inventiveness was in fact necessary in order to make usable social organizations that were adapted to the hard world of premodern Asia. The dysfunctional results of over-accurate genealogical recording were clearly exhibited in later Qing China, where the high level of record keeping and genealogical accuracy in fact burdened the empire with masses of impoverished and militarily ineffective hereditary soldiers.[26]

The establishment of formalized and durable states could result in genealogical fancies drifting free from effective lines of authority. The inhabitants of a medieval feudal kingdom might believe that they were descended from a single ancestor named Brut or Brit or Franco. That would not however, demarcate functioning patterns of authority or allegiance: the lord of the manor, the intermediate feudal lord, and, ultimately, the king were the real repositories of authority, while mythic ancestry was a jongleur's tale to while away a drunken evening in the Great Hall.[27]

Inner Asia: Chinggisid *Ulus* as Future Tribe

A few centuries after Chinese scholarship developed its new sociological term, the sweeping conquests of the Mongols both mobilized and shattered many steppe chiefdoms, agrarian kingdoms, and lesser communities. The Mongol Empire between ca. 1220 and 1300 was unquestionably the largest to have existed in Eurasia. Horse nomads were the military basis of its power. Pragmatically, Chinggis and his successors sought to redefine "Mongol" to mean a nomad subordinated to Chinggis's immediate genealogical network. Many Turkic groups were in fact so affiliated, but not all Mongolian speakers were.[28] "Mongol," viewed from the Chinggisid secretariat, was not an ethnicity, but a loyalty. This classification persisted under Chinggis's successors but with the Empire decentralized into four wings. The East Asian branch under Mongke and Khubilai completed the conquest of China in the decade after 1260. The Yuan imperial dynasty was established in China in 1271 and successfully extended its power over the south and southwest by subjugating northern Burma and Vietnam. Though immensely powerful, it was also short-lived; it was replaced in China by the Ming dynasty in 1368.[29]

"All who lived in felt tents" were drafted into Chinggis's armies. The term obviously referred to all those nomadic pastoralists whose traditional way of life had already accustomed them to small-band self-provisioning and mobile horse warfare. They were then grouped into units, shaped into armies, and moved— along with their families and flocks—wherever needed. If they conquered nomads capable of war, the latter too were allocated in numerically ordered bands—of ten, one hundred, one thousand, or ten thousand (the latter being the famous tuman). They were thus arbitrarily separated from their earlier social units, grouped into new collectivities, placed under the rule of particular Mongol leaders, and sent out to campaign wherever the great khans dictated. This is what Atwood refers to as the "appanage system."[30]

The appanages, or combinations of territories and subjects, allotted to the great princes of Chinggis's empire were officially termed *ulus*. Munkh-Erdene has published a deeply learned study of the deployment of that term in sources from the era of Mongol world empire. He denies that it can be translated as "tribe." Instead, he concludes that in Mongol records, the word was exclusively intended to mean "state." Furthermore, the term *ulus* only referred to Mongol organizations among all contemporary communities: others were referred to as *irgen*. So, Munkh-Erdene concludes, Mongol *ulus* denoted the Mongol people "after they were administratively organized."[31] That, however, would be how the organizers—which is to say, the ruling elite and their scribal dependents—used it. Ernest Gellner has shrewdly observed that "much of the evidence supporting the feudal interpretation comes from the imperial period of Mogol history..." This was a time when "a streamlined military organization was superimposed on the system of clans."[32] We should not assume that common speech among all those dragooned into the new formations possessed or retained the exactitude of secretariat practice.

The word certainly persisted through the generations even though the empire of Chinggis broke into segments and then into fragments. The term *ulus* traveled and changed with the Mongol conquests. It changed meaning as the social organization of the peoples using it devolved into an array of sociopolitical forms. The meaning of *ulus* was thus reconstituted by changing sets of loyalties and relationships in diverse regional and linguistic settings. Even among the far northwestern Mongol dependencies in forest zone Russia, *ulus* was adopted into medieval Russian as early as the mid-1300s. It was used by many Russian tributary princes to refer to their own kingdoms. Over the next two centuries, as the Mongol empire disintegrated, it moved down to refer to small nomadic units or administrative districts in the western lands of the Golden Horde, one of the four domains among the third-generation descendants of Chinggis.[33]

We should not, in fact, expect terminological clarity and stability. Mongol imperial records consulted by Munkh-Erdene reflected the preferences of empire builders. But the malleability of terms reflected the malleability of sociopolitical organizations. As Ouyang saw, communities were in flux, oscillating between consolidation and dispersion as they scattered and regrouped under the blows of man and nature. On the steppes, the pastoral "tribe" may be seen as the most common resulting form. It was a modal formation existing between the great but fleeting nomad empire and the small, enduring nomadic pastoral band. This entire range of social forms was, I argue, extant among those that used the grazing lands of the wide steppe from the Amur to the Dnieper. The confusion of indigenous categories is thus simply a reflection of the kaleidoscopic reality of the times.

Tribe in Iran and Iraq

The same terminological devolution had occurred within the Iranian conquests of the Mongols. Here the name was added to the mix of Arabic, Turkic, and Mongol names for durable sociopolitical groups. Richard Tapper could not find a clear Persian definition of ulus. Analysis, he wrote, "is not aided by the Persian terminology, including as it does a variety of words of Turco-Mongol and Arabic origins" (īl, ʿashīra, qabila, tīra, ṭaʾifa, uymaq and ulus), many of which have been used imprecisely and interchangeably. But Tapper adds that despite this terminological medley, the Iranian world possessed an understanding of the structural features of "tribe." A common basic feature of "tribal organization was a combination of notions of egalitarianism, individualism, independence and primary loyalty to paternal kinsmen; and that groups so based, under conditions of comparatively dense population and political autonomy, evolved larger, frequently militaristic confederations, while under conditions of strong government control they developed very different 'feudalistic' class structures."[34]

On the eastern borders of the Persian world, while researching the Hazara lands of northwestern Afghanistan, Ferdinand was told that before the subjugation of the region by the king of Afghanistan in the 1880s, tribal chiefs were titled "Khan." But important ones who could muster 2,000 horsemen used the old post-Chinggisid title of Il-Khan. This was understood as "the head of the ulus, the tribe or society."[35] We shall see that *ulus* definitively entered Indo-Persian usage when remote descendants of Chinggis established their own empire in North India, but, at least in the sixteenth century, it was used nearer to its ancient sense to label the armed followings of particular chieftains.

The ancient land of Mesopotamia lay at the western edge of the Mongol Empire. It was overrun by the Mongols who sacked Baghdad, the capital of the Islamic Caliphate, in 1258. Tribal organization persisted through this conquest as well as many later ones—Ottoman, British, and American. Iraq was a relatively late addition to the Ottoman empire. Ottoman rule there was contested by the Persian Shahs and subject to plundering incursions from the tribally organized deserts of the Arabian Peninsula. Hussain D. Hassan has described how under weak Ottoman rule, "Iraq's loose tribal confederations prevailed, with each tribe acting as a sort of mobile mini-state. Furthermore, in the absence of a strong central authority, the tribal framework fulfilled the primary functions of conflict and resource management." This tendency only intensified with the collapse of the empire following the First World War. The British took over the region, but, faced with a significant insurrection, began to cede power to tribal sheikhs in order to manage the country. During Iraq's first year of independence (1933), it was estimated that the country's central government had 15,000 rifles as against 100,000 similar weapons in the hands of various tribes. The minimal unit was the *khams*, which was composed notionally of every son descended from a given great-grandfather. A number of these were aggregated into an *ashira*, meaning "tribal organization." In 2007, Hassan observed that in contemporary Iraq, the latter could encompass from a few thousand up to over one million persons. A group of tribes formed a *qabila*, which in present-day Iraq is understood as a tribal confederation.[36] It is obvious that "tribal organization" here refers to widely different social units, from an identifiable cluster of lineages with a few thousand members, to what would elsewhere be an "ethnicity" or indeed a small nationality.

More than rifles, the key tribal asset was solidarity. This was manifested (as I have already mentioned) as late as 2014, when the expensively armed Iraqi army failed, and the desperate government turned to "the sons of the tribes." It is obvious that the Iraqi draftees of the regular army were also somebody's sons: the invocation of genealogy here clearly indicates that the minister believed in the reality of stable, identifiable, and long-lived social organizations, whose young men possessed a special military aptitude.

"Tribe" in Indic Social Thought

Southwest of China and southeast of Iran, the Indian subcontinent was home to another major Asian literate tradition. Early Indian political tradition also recognized distinct kinds of political formation. But the most important surviving text, titled the *Arthashastra*, is heavily monarchical in orientation. This summation of the early Sanskrit tradition was completed by the fourth century CE, perhaps under the Gupta Empire, and conceived as a manual for kingship.[37] It, however, devoted a chapter to what were clearly non-monarchical organizations. These were described as the most valuable allies and dangerous enemies. The *Arthashastra* was not deeply focused on empirical geography. Its assumed location appears, however, to be the central Gangetic Plain of North India. Significantly enough, the non-monarchical communities it discussed were located northwest and north of the Gangetic core. The former can be viewed as part of the West Asian arid zone, while the latter is one of the more humid regions of the subcontinent, intersected by many south-flowing rivers and possessing considerable forests.

The *Arthashastra* devoted a chapter of Book 11 to the management of *sanghas*—a word which has been variously translated as "corporation," "confederation," and "oligarchy." I argue that we should think of them as tribes. Of the rejected terms, "corporation" suggests a contractual unity, yet *sanghas* were clearly not short-term organizations, but intergenerational kin networks. The internal structure of these bodies is evident from the *Arthashastra*'s prescriptions for disrupting their unity. The chapter considers the ways in which such tribes might be conquered by the ambitious monarch. It advises against direct attack until internal feuds could be generated within these bodies. These feuds could be engineered by various devices. They included secret agents inciting lesser tribesmen to demand that the aristocrats should eat with and intermarry with them, while other agents incited the latter to refuse. If successful, the process would then lead to internal hatred and factionalism. The would-be conqueror should take one side so as to stimulate the broil. Divided, the community could thus be overcome by the aspirant to universal monarchy. The text clearly perceived the *sangha* as a long-lived social entity that maintained inter-generational familial ties. Its authors also visualized the tribe as already stratified, with distinctions of wealth and status between the great chiefs who sat in council and lesser tribesmen.

"Confederation" is also an unsatisfactory translation. It does not explain what the units that confederated were supposed to be: individuals, families or Swiss cantons, or why they might or might not eat together and marry into each others' families. Finally, we may consider 'oligarchy'. The *sanghas* might be described as oligarchical in their political structure, since they had councils of chiefs (and inciting quarrels among them was considered a valuable expedient). Stable tribes have indeed possessed such leadership. But "oligarchy" does not capture the relationship between rulers (the oligarchs) and the ruled. But an organized professional army to enforce the rulers' will would be needed for the society to be an oligarchic "state." The discussion of the *sangha* does not indicate there was any internal coercive force capable of overawing the entire community. The *Arthashastra* declared the *sangha* to be the best kind of ally because the mutual solidarity of its members made it impenetrable to enemies: that precludes the existence of a distinct coercive power within it, other than its own assembled warriors.

The text also distinguished between two different classes of tribe. The first lived by the "trade of war" (or by trade *and* war), and the compound describing them gives two regional names (Surashtra and Kamboja) that are broadly locatable to the west and northwest of the Gangetic Plain. They would have been entities like the "republics" described by the Greco-Roman historians of Alexander (who invaded India between 327 and 325 BCE). If the compound is (to my mind, implausibly) read as "trade and war," it is still comprehensible from later analogues of armed tribal caravans that moved seasonally through dangerous passes from the mountainous borderlands of the Indus Basin to the riverain plains of India. Alternatively, they were hill communities that extorted tolls from caravans passing by them: a practice that mutatis mutandis, still endures.

The second class of tribes analyzed in the *Arthashastra* were those described as living by the name "king." Historians have been puzzled by this phrase. But it is easily comprehensible in terms of their being privileged agrarian groups of a kind recognized even by the British colonial administration. These elites were sometimes genealogically connected to the local lord or simply regionally powerful. They were therefore allowed to pay lower rents or taxes. Their capacity for mutual assistance would help deter oppressive kings or tax collectors from infringing on their privileges. In effect, they were sharing the agrarian surplus with their overlords. The practice is attested even in the nineteenth and twentieth century. A British officer gave a vivid description of the reaction of one such privileged and militant group belonging to an inferior branch of a dominant lineage in North India in the 1870s when their lineage chief encroached on their privileges. Jymul Singh, a powerful landlord tried to raise their rents of "some illegitimate descendants of his grandfather" (i.e., lesser tribesmen of his own extended lineage). He went to the colonial civil courts to enforce his claims and got decrees from the Collector's and Judge's Courts. The losing defendants then waylaid Jymul Singh and his two brothers as they were coming back with their decree from the Judge's Court and "literally cut all three to pieces with tulwars [swords] and for this crime escaped all punishment for want of legal evidence against the culprits." The officer reporting this added that the "privileged tenants" of this Thakur community had generally been left undisturbed ever since.[38] One can cite many instances of such privileged tenure. I will cite an additional one.

Ajmer-Merwara was a British-ruled district in central Rajputana (now in the Indian state of Rajasthan). Much of it was held by fief-holders whom the colonial government had transformed into hereditary landlords. One such estate of twenty-seven villages was the fieldwork site of the anthropologist Ann Gold, who over several decades collected detailed oral histories under the rule of its last petty ruler, who was ousted in land reforms soon after India became independent in 1947. His caste-fellows were the Rajputs, the larger community after whom the region was named in medieval times. He had almost total power over the tenants on his lands but nonetheless allowed the Rajputs to pay only half the tax demanded of ordinary farmers.[39] These families were evidently living by the community identifier "Rajput" ("son of a king") as the *Arthashastra* would have described it.

Returning to the early centuries of the Common Era, communities analogous to the *Sangha* are addressed in the "Wisdom" books of the vast Sanskrit epic, the *Mahabharata*, probably written before 400 CE. The text did not label them sangha, however. The historian R. C. Majumdar has suggested that by the time the *Mahabharata* was completed, the word sangha was deeply associated with the Buddhist monastic order. So it uses a different word, *gana*, to describe this political formation. The *Mahabharata* chapter was more oriented to the defense of these tribal bodies. This book offered political advice to tribal *ganas*. In this instance, the advice concerned how they might resist disruption and maintain their unity. It emphasized the need for their leadership to avoid giving rise to jealousies and sustain the practice of having common assemblies and councils.

It advised the tribal folk (*gana*) to remain united, disregard malicious reports about each other, and thus protect their manly or military power. That unity would bring them wealth because outsiders would seek alliances with them. Indeed, we may see the recruitment of tribal auxiliaries by established kingdoms and aspirant conquerors occurring across Asia into the nineteenth century. The text especially warned their chiefs against greed and arrogance: these would lead to internal dissension and feuding. Of the two, arrogance was more dangerous because it inflamed everyone endlessly, while greed only angered the individual victim of chieftainly covetousness.[40] The *Arthashastra* did not exhaust the Indian political tradition, but even cursory consideration of the millennium between 500 and 1500 would extend this chapter into a full-length monograph. I therefore move to the Mughal Empire (ca. 1526–1700). The Mughal Empire in South Asia was effectively reorganized from the 1560s and began a systematic classification of its territories. A great compendium of information, titled *Ain-i-Akbari*, was completed by 1600. The empire made Persian its high administrative and court language. The seventeenth century, therefore, marked the high point of the Persianization of South Asian government. Many Persian-speaking soldiers and bureaucrats flocked into Mughal employment and brought the welter of post-Mongol social categories from Iran into India. By that time, indigenous observers and newcomers to South Asia alike perceived its society as composed of stable, hereditary corporate groups. As in Persia, authors used a medley of terms for all of them. These included the Arabic *qaum*, the Pashto *khail*, or sometimes the Persian *zat*. The Arabic *ahl* was occasionally used, as was the Turkic *il*.[41]

These terms were used for all kinds of durable social groupings that were arbitrarily differentiated as "tribe" and "caste" only in the late colonial period. Mughal authors did not analyze their genealogical (or other) basis. But they were separately classified according to their structures of authority. Reviewing documents and records from the reign of Akbar (1556–1605), the historian A. R. Khan found that chiefs were classified in two ways: either as rulers of named territories or as chiefs of a particular *alus* (*ulus*), which he translates as "clan" or "tribe." But he adds that this latter term was used only where the community also formed a well-knit military body, one that might originate in a kinship group mobilized as a military contingent. It was also used for a military contingent given the name of a kinship group. Many territorially organized kingdoms were controlled by the clan to which the ruler belonged, though they would constitute a minority privileged population (as in the Ajmer case above). *Ulus* were sometimes specifically described as hereditary groupings having several chiefs each of whom commanded segments of the tribe.[42]

The Mountain Massif and Archipelago of Southeast Asia

Between East and South Asia lie the mountains of the Southeast Asian Massif. Here we find a well-attested set of local descriptive terms whose denotations were explained by the influential British anthropologist Edmund Leach that we have discussed in the Introduction. Breaking from the academic tradition of imposing Western analytic categories, he consciously sought to deploy the ideas of the Kachin and Shan peoples in his region of study in order to classify their social systems. Later scholars have criticized his translation of Kachin terms. They have also contested his model of relatively stable oscillation between decentralized and autocratic forms of governance and argued for a greater similarity across the divide that he drew between republican and monarchic organization. But they agreed that his terminology was internal to the society that it described.[43]

Pocketing the hills were permanent rice farming communities on the valley floor termed Shan. Each of these formed a small feudal domain. Until the British decided that they had to enforce a separation between the Shan Valley chiefs and the upland Kachin villages, the latter were, in theory, dependencies of some Shan lordship.[44] These extended domains were locally termed *muang*. Echoing Leach, Jean Michaud described these domains as small monarchies, each centered on a town where the elite resided. The middle belt of the massif was dotted with such domains. Hundreds of placenames containing the word are found from Chinese Guanxi in the east to Indian Assam in the west.[45] Finally, there was a radical contempt of the residents of the two types of communities for each other, even though it was possible for branches of the same lineage to be *gumlao* and *gumsa*.[46]

In the swidden or fire-farming areas, a "village," Leach wrote, could be composed of even a single household, but the majority would have from ten to twenty households. The area over which villagers collectively had cultivation rights was demarcated by well-known landmarks, and villagers would move their tillage as the soil was exhausted. Leach, however, maintained that villages could shift from one social form to another and that relations with the valley floor lords could vary. Sometimes Kachin chiefs took tribute rather than paid it.

That there was clearly a contingent and historical dimension to the variations in social organization has been observed by other experts on the social organization and linguistics of the region. In this region of northern Burma, it appears that Asian societies did conceive of something like the modern idea of "tribal" political organization before they succumbed to the contemporary hegemony of Western categories. But the fieldwork was, of course, done in the twentieth century, in a time of British colonial rule and Christian missionary enterprise. It however fits with the concept of Southeast Asian Buddhist kingdoms as conceptually "galactic polities," with great areas of lightly governed or autonomous peoples, in contrast to tight controls at the royal centers.[47]

Leach's model, as widened by Tambiah, was also the pattern of the maritime regions of Southeast Asia. In 2002, Cynthia Chou and Geoffrey Benjamin summed up the results of a large, specialized conference on the tribal peoples of the "Malay world"—a culture region encompassing parts of Thailand as well as Malaysia and Indonesia. Benjamin's chapter in the book pointed to the long-term working of boundary-making processes in the region. The emergence of states commenced about two thousand years ago. Inhabitants were faced with the choice of becoming Malay peasants at the base of the social hierarchy or staying outside it while maintaining cultural and economic exchanges with emergent states. The growth of Chinese and Indian demand for specialized forest products paradoxically made foraging (gathering) more attractive than it had been. Three types of tribal identity and organization emerged around three lifeways—nomadic hunting-gathering, settled horticulture, and specialized collecting for long-distance exchange. Each of these, Benjamin argued, then locked into a specific kinship pattern that served as a cultural marker for the tribe. Entry required the establishment of recognized ties; exit was demonstrated by entering into impermissible relations.[48] The maintenance of a transgenerational system (which is what we call "kinship") requires the internalization of an understanding of appropriate and inappropriate relationships, and of inclusion and exclusion, which is to say, an image of self and other.

The Coming of European Categories

European powers arrived in the Indian Ocean after 1498. Portuguese, Dutch, and English observers initially labeled peoples they encountered "nations" or naçoes, used in the old sense of a descent group. They also applied gente or jente ("people," from the Latin gens) and the new Iberian coinage casta to describe the durable communities of Asia. With the rise of English, "race," "tribe," "clan," and "caste" were also indiscriminately used to label a variety of social groups. But starting with the Iberians in the Americas and Asia, Europeans were adding a biological concept of race to the mix. India was a British colony. It was easy for privileged

Englishmen to secure the help of the powerful colonial administration in their pursuits. In the nineteenth century, therefore, India, along with British Ceylon and Malaya, became a leading destination for those eager to collect animal heads or measure human ones. The same hapless peoples might indeed be conscripted as "beaters" to drive animals to the guns or to provide cranial measurements to test whatever theory their visitors wished to prove. Equally, the Asian intelligentsia began to assimilate Western theories that came with all the weight of imperial dominance behind them. The next chapter will examine the history of Western ideas of "tribe" in Asia.

2

HOW THE "TRIBE" CAME TO ASIA

"[W]hen I speak of the great divisions of the Aufghans, I shall call them tribes."

— Elphinstone, 1842

Academic discourse—and the global public sphere of which it forms an infinitesimal part—were both shaped by European powers for two centuries. Even today, the centers of media imaging and academic discourse still reside in the so-called "North." We must, therefore, begin with a history of the term "tribe" in the Latin West after the sixteenth century, before transitioning to its application to Asian social groups in English and French.

As is well-known, *tribus* is an old Latin noun, originally applied to the divisions of the people among the ancient Romans. These tribes possessed internal governments headed by their "tribune" and took their disputes to the "tribunal." It has been suggested that *tribus* was originally a compound meaning "the three peoples" or "three orders." Latin was the language of learning across the European world into the nineteenth century. The word *tribus* entered many European languages during the medieval period. In English, we find it in a 1752 thesaurus. It was used (in translations from Hebrew) as a name for the twelve divisions of the people of Israel described in Exodus and elsewhere.[1] After the Christian religious schism of the 1530s, the Protestant churches pushed to translate the Bible from Greek and Hebrew into English. These new vernacular texts obviously popularized the word "tribe," among all English-speakers, to refer to a closed descent group with a hypothetical single male ancestor.

The Catholic world initially did not adopt the new term in its vernacular sociology, either in the Americas or Asia. The Portuguese controlled all seaborne

European access to the Indian Ocean for almost a century. Asian ships never went West, and in the Indian Ocean they also largely sailed under stringent conditions that came with Portuguese permits. Crucially, the Portuguese arrived at the beginning of the print revolution in the West. Their control of communication channels also controlled the diffusion of content. Western knowledge of Asia was therefore mediated through Portuguese (and for the learned, Latin). Portuguese became a *lingua franca* around the littoral. But the social category of "tribe" (*tribus*) was rarely used by the Portuguese, despite their Latin heritage. Other than *casta*—a racially tinged sociological term common to both Portuguese and Spanish empires—communities were usually called *gente* or *jente*, or *nacione* or *naçoe*. All four words referred to a specific "people" in the loosest sense of this last term.[2]

Early English Use

But the Portuguese seaborne empire declined, and the British gradually grew into the major South Asian colonial power. They dominated the Indian Ocean throughout the nineteenth century. The British adopted "caste" from the Portuguese but initially used it as loosely as "tribe." Their frequent use of "tribe" likely came from Anglophone Protestants' familiarity with the English Bible, which they heard regularly in church services and read privately too. But the term was still loosely used to mean an ethno-political grouping. We, therefore, find great nomenclatural confusion in early English documents. The English East India Company took over the formerly Portuguese-ruled island of Bombay in 1665, and a few years later, the governor wrote to his superiors that there were several different "nations" (also described as "orders or tribes") inhabiting it. (I have modernized the orthography in the quote below by expanding abbreviations, but not changed spellings.)

> [I]n order to preserve the Govern[ment] in constant regular method, free from that confusion which a body composed of so many nations will be subject to, it were requisite [that] [the] severall nations at pres[ent] inhabiting or hereafter to inhabit on the Island of Bombay be reduced or modelled into so many orders or tribes, & that each nation may have a Cheif [*sic*] or Consull of the same nation appointed over them by the Gover[nor] and Councell.

It is evident that the governor thought of "tribe" as an enduring but malleable political unit, shaped and managed but not invented by the state. "Nations" were diverse, but their governance required that they be organized under headmen who would act as their representatives and heads. This was achieved: at any rate, the governor's grand procession was accompanied by the chiefs of the fifteen "orders or tribes." These included Catholic, Parsi, Hindu, and Muslim communities. Right through the eighteenth century, the East India Company's government referred a range of disputes to the "heads of the casts" for reporting and recommendation.

The distinctive twentieth-century anthropological contraposition of "tribe" and "caste" was still absent as late as the 1820s. For example, in 1823, Thomas Marshall, reporting to the government of Bombay, wrote of one district: "the Weavers are either of the tribe of Lingayut [a religious community] or of another Kanaree tribe called Hutgur." Today, both of these would be classified as "castes." He went on: "the tribe of Bunyas [a generic term for all Hindu and Jain merchant castes] educated to reading and accompts being unknown here." To add to the confusion, any descent group could also be labeled "race"—so Marshall writes, "a respectable Mahratta [today both an ethnonym and a caste-name] (to which race the institution is confined)." From North India in the same period, we find two Muslim communities self-classified as Sheikh [Arabic title meaning "chief"; used in India by many Muslims as a status label] and Sayyad [descendant of the Prophet] that are referred to as *races*. "The village is divided into two [sections], corresponding with the two races [*sic*] by which it is occupied."[3] This ethnographic looseness, however, had little administrative effect. Its practical unimportance is why it was allowed to persist.

But some officials began to realize that tribal organization framed political life in at least some parts of Southern Asia. Diplomacy and governance, then, required them to understand how it worked. The British also created a large bureaucratic machine, designed to function stably through changes of personnel over years and generations. That required the creation of a stable, legible body of records. So after social categories became administrative and political ones, it became necessary to both label and describe them exactly.

The earliest systematic effort at developing a typology of tribal social organization was published by the English statesman Mountstuart Elphinstone in 1815. His account was based on the collective research of a delegation that was sent by the East India Company to the court of the king of Afghanistan, Shah Shuja, 1808–09. The Shah was suspicious of their intentions. They were not allowed to cross west of the Khyber Pass. The Shah met them at the border town of Peshawar, where a treaty of friendship was signed. He was shortly thereafter overthrown by his half-brother, and fled into exile in Panjab. The delegates, however, canvassed the court during their visit and spoke with travelers and sojourners. Elphinstone also visited some of the Afghan settlements in North India in order to understand the people the English planned to enlist as allies of the East India Company against a feared Franco-Russian overland invasion. Like all reported accounts of unvisited lands, it may therefore be somewhat idealized and schematic.

Elphinstone, however, realized something that later scholarship has confirmed. Tribal organization along purportedly genealogical lines constituted the functional frame of Afghan society. Each tribe was, he wrote, a "commonwealth in itself." It was, he argued, far more durable than the dynasty of the moment.[4] Any future British dealings with the Afghans—including perhaps the extension of British hegemony there—would depend on an accurate understanding of the dynamics of the system. He therefore sought analytic exactitude. Analyzing the political organization of the Afghans in the early nineteenth century he wrote, "I beg my readers to remark, that hereafter, when I speak of the great divisions of the Afghauns, I shall call them tribes; and when the component parts of a tribe are mentioned with reference to the tribe, I shall call the first divisions clans: those which compose a clan, Khails, &c, as above." He clearly distinguished independent units from their subordinate parts. So he added that "when I am treating of one of those divisions as an *independent* body, I shall call it Oolooss, and its component parts clans, khails, &c, according to the relation they bear to the Oolooss [ulus] as if the latter were a tribe."[5]

A hundred and fifty years after Elphinstone, a team of Danish anthropologists reported that "[a]part from the Tajik population, everybody in Afghanistan belongs to a more definite ethnic group, mostly a tribal group with a more or less fixed structure. A common Afghan proverb is: 'A Hazāra without a *Dāy*, is as an Afghan without a – *zai*,' which means, that it is just as unthinkable to meet a Hazāra who does not belong to a particular tribe as it is to meet a de-tribalized Afghan."[6] Mountstuart Elphinstone and other educated upper-class men like him were at the interface of the learned worlds of Europe and Asia. They read the thinkers of the Enlightenment and supplied the learned societies of Europe with much of their firsthand information about Asia. But they also created a new imperial administration out of the failures of the military-commercial structure of the eighteenth-century East India Company. With them, colonial sociology grew from a grab bag of names and ideas into a systematic effort to understand social structure in order to change it. The efforts by Elphinstone—who was then a middle-ranking official—to develop an unambiguous classification of Afghan sociopolitical structure was a part of that effort.

The French Colonial Empire

France was the other international empire that dominated metropolitan scholarship in the period when "tribe" was acquiring its sociological meaning. The French language also inherited *tribu* from Latin. So it was a term applied to the study of antiquity—the Romans and ancient Jews were described as divided into these classes. A *tribu* was anciently "a thirty-fifth portion of the people of Rome . . . . we may term these thirty-five 'bands' or 'leagues' or 'cantons.' . . . Each had its own name and there was no Roman citizen who was not affiliated to one of these thirty-five bands or tribes." It is notable that Jean Nicot's modern (1606) comparisons were to "bands" of soldiers, bandits, or merchants, or to *cantons*—a term that was coming to mean "districts."[7] It crops up in the writing of the early French in South Asia too. François Martin was governor of the settlement at Pondicherry and lived in India for over thirty years. In 1683, he used the label *tribu* to describe Hindu merchants (*baneanes*).[8]

The French were academic as well as political rivals of the British in "Oriental studies." The French scientific expedition into Egypt (1798) caused a stir in the European academy. In 1806 the English scholar James Mackintosh addressed the Literary Society of Bombay and encouraged its members to emulate French overseas scholarship. The academic establishments of the two empires were thus always aware of each other.[9] The early nineteenth century was a time when the new social sciences were taking shape. Aspirations to science, as well as legal and administrative processes, required the development of unambiguous taxonomy. "Tribe"—despite French reluctance to use it—was soon an important term within the still largely armchair field of anthropology, whose authors relied on the reports of stray travelers and colonial officials.

There was lively academic rivalry and debate among the learned in England and France through the eighteenth and nineteenth century. It is probably as a result of this interaction that academic French began to use *tribu* as a sociological category. A search of JSTOR for French articles found mentions of the word contemporary to parallel English scholarship. In this instance, French use of the term referred to the Americas, Asia, and North Africa. It assumed that precolonial social organization in the Ohio Valley, for example, had consisted of "unknown tribes." Likewise, an early study of the Khalka Mongols similarly identified them as "independent tribes of pastoral warriors."[10] A few decades later, the political formations of interior North Africa in the time of French colonization were also identified as *tribus*.[11]

In the last case, this was obviously a translation of the Arabic *qabileh*, from which the geographical name "Kabylie" ("land of tribes") was derived. But notably, as with Indic names available to the British to describe local social organization, there was no effort at using *qabileh* as a loanword in French analysis. It only appeared so as to provide an etymology for the regional name "Kabylie" in the 1877 dictionary.[12] Twentieth-century French scholarship also did not favor the term for colonized Asian communities. Drawing from Oscar Salemink, Charles Keyes notes that anthropologists in French Indochina "used various terms such as *race, sauvages, populations, peuplades*, and, occasionally, *tribu*. The term *montagnard* ["man of the mountains"] was used specifically for upland-dwelling peoples."[13] *Tribu* was, however, frequently used by some French writers, such as Henri Maitre, author of *Les Regions Moïs*, in 1909, as, for example, when he translated the ethnic term *Raglais* as "man of the woods," adding that they were a "*tribu des sauvages de la montagne*" ("a tribe of mountain-dwelling savages").[14] This was part of what became a widespread "evolutionist" discourse. It was part of a "Social-Darwinian fascination for the 'survival of the fittest' [that] would be a recurring theme in French evolutionists' texts on the Montagnards."[15] Habitat as refuge and cultural primitivism were thus conflated in the general term *Montagnard*.

Racial Anthropology and the "Tribe"

From the mid-nineteenth century, the emerging discipline of anthropology, although unequipped with a scientific genetics, nonetheless began to derive sociocultural traits from supposedly immutable physical ones. The middle decades of the nineteenth century were a time when geology led the way in undermining the foundations of Biblical chronology and, indirectly, Biblical monogenism. The popularity of geology caused it to serve as a model for "race theory." That in turn soon grew into the cutting-edge "Theory" of its time and helped to shape the study of humanity for a century thereafter. John Hunt, president of the Anthropological Society and a leading racial theorist, enunciated the social scientist's aspiration to rock-hard certitude in 1863:

> [if] any plea were wanting for founding this [anthropological] society, I would ask you to look at the different degrees of progress which the sciences of Geology and Anthropology have made during the last fifty years. . . . Geology has within a few years become a great science and the most ignorant or superstitious dare not assail her conclusions.

In this gradually hardening theory, "races" were formed like geological strata, with the earlier lying beneath the later. It was a doctrine naturally appealing to late-arriving colonizers the world over.

The British Empire in India was the forge where British political anthropology shaped its conceptual tools. Charles Grant wrote the first (and therefore much-replicated) *Gazetteer* (official handbook) of Central India soon after it became a full-fledged province of British India. He composed a conjectural history of the Gond community, now an Indian "Scheduled Tribe." He speculated that:

> they were as little fitted to cope with men of Aryan descent in peace as in war; and though slow centuries of enervation under an Indian sky had relaxed the northern vigour of the races to whom they had once before succumbed, yet in every quality and attainment which can give one people superiority over another, there was probably as much difference between Hindus and Gonds as there is now between Anglo-Americans and Red Indians, or between Englishmen and New Zealanders [Maori]. . . . Those of the aborigines who remained were absorbed, though never so

completely as to attain equality with the people who had overrun them. They form at present, the lowest stratum of the Hindu social system, allowed to take rank above none but the most despised outcastes.

A decade later, the important colonial official Bartle Frere also argued that while some communities were indeed disappearing, others might ultimately be fitted into an ethnic hierarchy. Select elites might even actually beacculturated to the British imperial system.[16] Frere both used analogies to ancient empires such as Rome and illustrated his ideas from his administrative charge in British India. Speaking before the Anthropological Society in 1882, he declared:

> [t]here is much to justify the conjecture that each caste marks a separate conquest of some aboriginal tribe, each tribe having had its separate work assigned to it in the organisation of the village community . . . till the European Aryan with his roads and railroads, his uniform codes and his centralized administration broke into the aboriginal reserve of the Warlis and Bhils, of Sonthals or Gonds or Koles, [all communities now on the list of tribes recognized by the Government of India] and in half a generation effected more change than Hindu Rajas or Moslem Nawabs had effected for centuries before him.

Only the energy of the British could, in Frere's view, replicate the civilizing impact of the Romans throughout their empire and gradually uplift all its peoples to the maximum that their capacities permitted. The historical fantasy, therefore, was that an "Aryan" people had preceded the British and had successfully conquered a succession of aboriginal tribes. Each of the latter was believed to have been incorporated as a caste. These mythic Nordic conquerors stacked conquered tribes into occupationally divided village communities. Only a few tribes survived this process, and they did so by retreating into individual refuges. There was thus a continuity between tribe and caste. Between them, "tribe" and "caste" were deemed to exhaust the social imagination of traditional India before the British. Surviving aboriginal tribes retreated into remote and inhospitable areas. But their character could assume two forms: recalcitrant ferocity or refugee timidity.[17]

Contradictory Psychologies of Tribalism

Twentieth-century French analysts in North Africa also made a stylized distinction between the character of the submissive peoples of the *bled al-makhzen* and the recalcitrance of those in the *bled as [al] siba*. Men in the latter category, Celerier wrote in 1936, did not depend on the external authority of the Sultan of Morocco to safeguard either their persons or their property. They relied on the armed solidarity of their village community and their tribe. Each man was correspondingly ready to rally violently to the side of his paternal kin in any conflict with outsiders, without regard to the justice of the cause. Tillers of the soil, he added, were submissive to authority; pastoralists were militant.[18] Celerier was echoing an old stereotype. As we have seen, across much of the world, "tribalism" carried and carries a connotation of an irrational solidarity accompanied by a readiness for violence. The idea is represented in postcolonial India by, for example, V. Raghaviah, whose book includes laudatory prefaces by the President and Vice President of India. Raghaviah declared that "the tribals are the children of the jungles, they are the flowers of the forest." But they lived there because they had been "unjustly driven into these unwholesome, unwelcome mountain fastnesses by ruthless invading hordes superior in numbers *as in their brain power.*"[19]

The Republic of India (but not that of Pakistan) had an additional concept of the psychology of "tribal peoples" that also arose from the colonial narrative. If tribal peoples were primitive, threatened refugees from "ruthless invading hordes," and they were consequently shy. The idea that comportment manifests identity has, in recent decades, been reverse engineered by the government of India to make a certain behavior ("shyness") a requirement for recognition as a legally extant tribe.[20] So two flatly contradictory models emerged here. One was that of tribes as "shy primitives," living fossils practically, peoples who needed paternal colonial protection from other Asians.

The other concept was of "tribes" as fierce and ungovernable folk who could only be kept in check by demarcating a special area within which they could govern themselves. In this latter case, raids or other transgressions of the border could only be checked by collective punishments and the destruction of the production base of tribal society. This was the *razzia* (indiscriminately destructive raid) form of governance pioneered by the French Marshal Bugeaud in the "tribal lands" (or lands of the Kabyles) of French colonial Algeria in the nineteenth century. The method of collective punishment was also applied by the British well into the twentieth century against the tribes of the Afghanistan-Pakistan borderland and also on the periphery of the Zomia mountain massif in Eastern India. Areas of Southeast Asia that fell outside the empire were also deeply influenced by Western theory. This was the period when social thought across Asia was being "racialized."[21]

In the French and British Empires alike, it was also assumed that many "lower" races were doomed to disappear upon the arrival of their European superiors. The English founder of racial anthropology, John Hunt, and the French anthropologist Paul Topinard were contemporaries. The latter worked for many years in the museum of natural history in Paris and had a founding role in French race theory. At the same time, the highly influential social anthropologist Lewis H. Morgan developed beyond this static (and racist) analysis. He used savagery and barbarism as analytic categories and not mere terms of abuse. In his view, savagery was the lowest and longest stage of human society, but one out of which barbarian society evolved. The latter then created the conceptual and technical bases from which civilization emerged.

Morgan's ideas were developed by Marx and Engels to argue that "savagery" was in fact the universal early condition of humanity, "primitive communism," an anticipation of what a future society would achieve at a far higher level of culture. These ideas proved immensely influential across the world, not least in Asia. In the received version of Marxism-Leninism, each of Marx's stages (or modes of production) included a pattern of production, of interaction with "man's inorganic body," the earth.[22] Twentieth-century Western anthropologists avoided invoking Marx but maintained the notion of foraging (hunting and gathering), shifting agriculture (including swidden), and settled permanent farming as successive stages of progress. Foragers and shifting agriculturists were thought to live in egalitarian, "tribal" societies; settled farmers were on the path to creating organized chiefdoms and, ultimately, states.[23]

By World War I, the idea that "tribal" social organization reflected the backward and aboriginal traits of the people who had adopted it was widespread in the academy. It also reflected the dominance of racial theories in the West. Caste's conceptual twin was then the idea of "tribe." This would be a group defined as "primitive" and "isolated": that was why it had *not* become a caste. The theory that forest tribes had fled into the woodlands as a consequence of the advance of "superior races" was particularly appealing to Western scholars who were seeking pure specimens of ancient races. If the hypothesis of their age-long isolation was correct, then here was the solution to the problem bewailed by the leading French anthropologist Topinard, that "the interesting types [were] disappearing before our eyes; mixings and crossings . . . increasing to disastrous levels."[24]

In the colonial era, all these terms also had strong racial overtones. Some groups (the colonial officer Charles Grant wrote in 1870) could not be given the "polish" needed to make them suitable members of a civilization. The metaphor refers to an intrinsic quality of some types of stone; so "unpolishability" was clearly perceived as a racial trait. As I have shown elsewhere, the tribe/caste binary emerged out of late colonial racial ethnology, which then transformed Indian society's understanding of itself.[25] The concept of the primitive tribe hardened with the adoption of "tribe" or "aboriginal tribe" in the all-India censuses that began in 1881. It gradually began to shape colonial policy and legislation. Men such as Bartle Frere and Charles Grant were influential policymakers across the British Empire. Their views inevitably shaped the modernizing administrative apparatus of the later nineteenth century.

In Sri Lanka, the Vedda community of swidden farmers and hunters were identified as a relic of the "Stone Age." Viewing them became an item on the colonial tourist trail in upland Sri Lanka, just as "protecting" them has become a progressive cause in the present. The Seligmanns observed tourism by 1911. "The white man appeared to be immensely anxious to see a true Vedda, a wild man of the woods, clad only in a scanty loin cloth, carrying his bow and arrows on which he depended for his subsistence, simple and untrained, indeed, little removed from the very animals he hunted." The Seligmanns described the parading of suitably "made up" Veddas by local headmen. When summoned, they would appear in scanty clothing with tousled hair, though otherwise dressing like ordinary Sinhala villagers.[26]

Race theory, along with much other Western science, was adopted by many in the colonial intelligentsia across South Asia. Obeyesekere has described this for Ceylon (Sri Lanka). The first Reader in Ethnology appointed by the University of Calcutta directly connected extant "tribal" groups with the earliest Paleolithic inhabitants of the subcontinent. He clearly viewed them as biologically distinct and unchanged.

> Their spoor [sic] may be everywhere followed from the flat-faced, curl-haired Koch of Assam with thick protuberant lips of the Negro to the dark and irregularly featured Nepalese, to the Santhals of Chota Nagpur as also the low-caste hillmen of Southern India. They might justly be regarded as the unimproved descendants of the manufacturers of the stone implements found in the Damodar coal-fields.

"Depressed Classes" and "Aboriginal Tribes" began to be administratively recognized by the Government of India in the 1890s. Their "protection" was also a suitable ideological rejoinder to Indian critics of empire, a proof of its love for the oppressed. Special inner frontiers were instituted for the aboriginal tribes in parts of British India, and outsiders prohibited from crossing these. On the other hand, a special legal regime was created for "turbulent" tribal zones. Benjamin Hopkins recently showed how a new "tribal law" regime was created soon after the British annexation of Panjab. It then served as a model for similar legislation in colonial Africa and Palestine.

This law was the Frontier Crimes Regulation, first introduced in 1872. It formalized counterinsurgency practices already current in much of the colonial world. It thus provided for the collective punishment of offenses, which was to be inflicted on the community to which the malefactor was believed to belong. That punishment—which might include the seizure of property—was intended to induce tribal or village chiefs to surrender the culprit, pay fines (sometimes levied in firearms), or compensate the victim.[27] It was, as Hopkins has written, "predicated on ideas of space and governance common throughout much of upland Asia, as well as similarly situated 'borderland' regions around the globe. Many to whom the Regulation and its Kenyan counterpart applied had much in common with the inhabitants of 'Zomia'—upland Southeast Asia."[28] In fact, the British government also maintained an "Inner Line" frontier around its own "Zomia" region in the northeast, and the policy was only gradually eased in recent decades.

But another, and very different, kind of "tribe" was also recognized by the colonial government. Membership in it carried serious disadvantages. We have noted that by the late nineteenth century, colonial policy began to classify the diverse population of South Asia into watertight compartments. These included "Criminal Tribes," families that allegedly committed crimes as a family and "tribal" tradition. They were thought to permeate settled society, both urban and rural. In 1871, the British government passed special legislation, giving the police in North India special powers over them. In 1911, this was widened across British India, and the authorities had special extrajudicial powers of detention and control over communities listed under the Criminal Tribes Act. Communities so defined were deemed to be "criminals by birth" who had to be forcibly settled and reformed. That process involved requiring them to inhabit particular settlements. One such settlement was created near the town of Sholapur, and its residents had to work in the cotton mills that were coming up in the city.[29]

The colonial administrative apparatus was more firmly established east of the mountains, in the plains and open valleys of the Panjab. The greater Indus Valley area was economically important and politically sensitive. Much of the British Indian Army that sustained the empire, from Suez to Singapore and beyond, was recruited there. Even though the government did not allow complete tribal autonomy in Panjab, yet it strove to adapt to regional structure and traditions. At the time of the British conquest, corporate brotherhoods controlled many villages, and tribal chieftains sometimes dominated large tracts. British rule enhanced the power of law courts and, consequently, of the moneylenders who knew how to work them. Landowners large and small began to lose their land. The issue was economically and politically vital in the Panjab. By the end of the nineteenth century, its peasantry underpinned a military apparatus that held the British Empire east of Suez together. It was politically vital to buttress small farmers without alienating the dominant gentry either.

This triangulation was attempted by the Land Alienation Act of 1900. It did so by inventing a radically different concept of tribe. Tribes as recognized by the law were not different from peasants: they too lived in land-owning farming communities. Under the Act, landowners were to be classified as either "Agricultural" or "Non-Agricultural"—a division wholly absent from anthropological theory or administrative practice before this. The act provided a long list of "tribes"—Hindu, Muslim, and Sikh alike, that were deemed to be "Agriculturists" and hence specially protected by legislation against the transfer of their land to "Non-Agriculturist" tribes. Inclusion in either list was an unabashedly political decision. As P. J. Fagan, deputy commissioner of Hoshiarpur, wrote in 1901:

> Our decision as to any particular tribe must turn largely on political considerations. The whole Act itself is confessedly an attempt to check results which naturally flow from the educational, legal and fiscal systems which we have established in this country. The main pretext for such action is the political danger of the expropriation of the agricultural tribe, and therefore before a tribe is declared agricultural and brought within the direct scope of the Act, it seems proper to consider whether its numbers, position, etc., *render it of sufficient political or social importance to be considered an agricultural tribe.* (emphasis added)

Creditor members of an "agricultural tribe" could acquire the land of other members through mortgage and foreclosure. Nonmembers, who might also be owed money, could not. As result, there was soon much litigation around the membership of the new "tribes." Exasperated by it, the Panjab government amended the law so that the district executive officer's power to label any particular individual as "agricultural" was placed beyond all legal challenge.[30] As this was a cynically invented category, I will omit it from the argument hereafter.

Thus, the same word has comfortably accommodated three opposing assumptions about "tribal psychology": the tribe as militant, meek, and merely criminal. In British India, the concept of the "tribe militant" was used to characterize the northwest of the empire, the borderlands of Afghanistan. The stereotype also applied to several hill communities of the north-east. In other regions, the colonial government developed a model of the tribe as a primitive refugee community, fleeing the power of agrarian civilization and therefore in need of protection by the benevolent colonial state. The idea of racial traits was never far behind: the inferior were fleeing before the superior. Members of the tribe were therefore shy and retiring. Whatever the implicit psychological model may be, it is yet noteworthy that the correlation of affective trait and organizational concept was and is continually sought to be established.

The Post-Imperial Legacy in South and East Asia

The new governments of India, Pakistan, and Sri Lanka all inherited parts of the late imperial administrative apparatus, its law codes, and personnel. The category "tribe" was retained by the governments of India and Pakistan for their own administrative purposes. In India, the term was enshrined in the constitutional schedule or list of protected communities. Different states of the Indian union were tasked with compiling lists of tribal communities that deserved such protection. But such use in turn triggered contemporary political mobilizations around it.

In the middle years of the 1970s, for example, the government of India began an energetic effort to undo previous transfers of land from "tribal" to "non-tribal" ownership. That in turn motivated many rural inhabitants to assert a "tribal" identity in order to preclude challenges to their land titles.[31] After 1947, the successor government of Pakistan also maintained the administratively distinct tribal zone for many decades.

Meanwhile, Anglo-American social anthropology, whence the hand-me-down term "tribe" had come, became increasingly skeptical of its validity. The term was robustly challenged by Edmund Leach in 1954. That year, Leach published the previously cited intensive study of "tribal" communities in upland Burma. His argument comprehensively rejected the idea that either language or biology differentiated the three major types of political community that he identified in Northern Burma (now Myanmar).[32] Fredrik Barth was simultaneously studying another set of borderland communities—the Pathans (or Pakhtuns) as well as the adjoining Baluch of the Pakistan-Afghanistan borderlands. He too developed an understanding of "tribe" as a product of political ecology and history. But as a consequence of colonial conceptual spillovers, people on the periphery of independent agrarian states like the Thai kingdom were also perceived as racially alien and primitive; in short, conforming to the Western model of a tribe.

In China itself, the long-standing sense of cultural superiority briefly took on a racial tinge under the shattering impact of Western power. Dikötter wrote that the notion of a Han race emerged in a relational context of opposition both to foreign powers and to the ruling Manchus. Race was now "deemed to be an objective, universal and scientifically observable given." But for the revolutionaries, "the notion of a 'yellow race' was not entirely adequate as it included the much reviled Manchus." Whereas the reformers perceived race (*zhongzu*) as a biological extension of the lineage (*zu*), encompassing all people dwelling on the soil of the Yellow Emperor, some revolutionaries excluded the Mongols, Manchus, Tibetans, and other population groups from their definition of nationality. The Chinese nation was narrowed down to the Han, who were referred to as a *minzu*, a term imported from Japan.

Minzu was a new composite term meaning literally "people-lineage," and it was often used to translate the term "nation" and "nationality." Dikötter (and other scholars) have observed that the introduction and growth of the social sciences in China occurred as a response to the challenge posed by the West. This was as true for eminent progressive scholars and revolutionaries in the past, such as Liang Qichao, Cai Yuanpei, and Mao Zedong, as it was for leading intellectuals at later times. In the May Fourth Movement of 1919 and the New Culture Movement in the 1910s and 1920s, "science" was considered one of the root causes of the West's military and economic superiority over China.[33]

As a result, as Pieke described, the ranked ethnic concept of nationhood took deep root in China. The Communist Party of China now defines the People's Republic as a multinational nation-state. Unlike South Asia, however, the characterization of minority nationalities did not class them as having—or having had—a distinct type of social organization, the "tribe." "All citizens are unambiguously assigned to one or the other specific group, either the majority Han Chinese, or else one among the fifty-five minority nationalities."[34]

We have already considered the concept of the "tribe militant" in journalistic discourse and security studies. But an alternative discourse, that of the "tribe" as victim, has also percolated through other arms of the Western policy establishment. The determination of whether specific communities were in fact "tribal" according to the World Bank's definition of the term became very significant for the bank's decisions on funding the Narmada Dam Project in Western India in the 1990s. Reviewing the dam debate, the political scientist John Woods automatically translated *adivasis* (a Hindi neologism, meaning "original inhabitants") as "tribal people."

Advocates across Asia began to "dress up" the communities whose protection they sponsored. The Vadda of Sri Lanka (British-era Ceylon) had long been accustomed to being presented as specimens of the "Stone Age." Gananath Obeyesekere observed this being invoked once again. He commented that a picture by Viveca Stegborn, a Vadda rights activist, that had appeared in the *New York Times*, "showing Vaddas of Maha Oya carrying bows and arrows and in a stalking posture must very likely have been posed to convey the idea of 'indigenous people' living close to nature and now being threatened by extermination—a hugely successful ploy as far as the UN committee on the rights of indigenous people were concerned."[35]

The 1990s also saw a UN conflation of "tribal" with "indigenous," which was then conflated with "minority" of any kind. A veteran Indian anthropologist noted caustically that in China, this resulted in 2,900 Russians being described as the indigenous people of China: the Han however, were not deemed to be so.[36] Comment is superfluous. The concept of tribe has remained "good to think" and, correspondingly, expedient to deploy.

3

THE POLITICAL ECOLOGY
OF TRIBAL LIFE

*"It should be known that differences in condition among people are
the result of the different ways in which they make their living."*

— Ibn Khaldun, *Muqaddimah*

The Concept of Political Ecology

Environmental determinism is an old doctrine in social thought. But in the
early model, humans were shaped by a relatively stable environment. Among
ecologists, a radical theoretical shift came in the 1970s with the adoption of
nonlinear systems (the famous "butterfly effect"), the acceptance of the possibility
of multiple possible equilibria and others. But implicit equilibrium models have
survived more strongly in the social sciences. Much writing still accepted "that—at
least in the past—balanced, harmonious, and traditional systems existed, but that
these had been disrupted by the forces of modem change."

Discarding that idea, however, has freed analysts to consider various human
ways of managing their biosphere as equally valid. The long history of human
landscape modification is now being understood not as destruction, but as an
effort at creating a usable habitat for the social group in question. If the society
was sociopolitically unequal, landscapes would change as the will of the powerful
and the resistance of the subordinated played out through historical time.[1]

But how does the concept of "tribe" fit in this frame? The reader may recollect
that I am attempting to extract the rational historical kernel from the variously
colored pop-cultural shells that enclose the term. I have therefore suggested that

we see tribes as forms of weakly centralized (or widely diffused) power. Following the last retreat of the glaciers ten millennia ago, all of the humanized earth was governed by these, or yet simpler, regimes. Things dramatically changed with the rise of kingdoms and empires that began about four thousand years ago. Their aggressive expansion pushed various peoples to emulate, escape, or resist them. Major concentrations of power needed to support bodies of privileged full-time specialists—professional soldiers to enforce the ruler's authority, but also scribes to record, accountants to manage, and priests to sanctify its exercise. As Ibn Khaldun observed, some habitats were more easily adapted to such purpose, while others were utterly unusable for it. But between these hard limits, there existed a contested range of habitats amenable to various uses. Some of these uses were refractory to the centralized state and hierarchical society that came with it.

But the intensity and pattern of human environmental manipulation reflected patterns of authority and subjection within the human groups modifying it. The recalcitrant moved to terrain that was difficult for external authorities to surveil, penetrate, and control. They then shaped the land to suit their lifeway. States variously cleared forests, drained swamps, irrigated deserts, and built great walls to conquer, to contain, or to exclude ungovernable peoples. These are all processes of political ecology. The rest of this chapter will present concrete cases of such processes.

The Political Ecology of Asia

The ecological map of Asia (Map 2) shows that much of geographical Asia is too cold, too hot, or too dry for its biomass output to dependably support large, dense human populations. The greatest potential in terms of the combination of temperature and rainfall is evidently in East and Southeast Asia. But much of the latter region is then limited by its ruggedness. The extensive Zomia uplands offered possibilities for escape from the exactions and oppressions of states.[2] But fields had to be small and widely spaced unless huge amounts of labor were expended to build and maintain terraced fields. On the other hand, lands within the Great Wall (or agrarian China) were both significantly moister and comparatively flatter than the predominant landscapes of West or South Asia. West Asia outside Mesopotamia had only islands of tillage among vast arid and semiarid lands best used for nomadic pasture. South Asia ecologically merged into the arid zone of Southwest Asia but had more rain as well as seasonally rising rivers. Such agricultural areas were nonetheless interspersed with arid zones: only the main Gangetic Plain provided generally adequate natural rainfall for cereals as well as level land for plough tillage. Historically, across the subcontinent, there were also areas of modified woodland or pastoral savanna that were more a product of climatic fluctuation or political vicissitude.

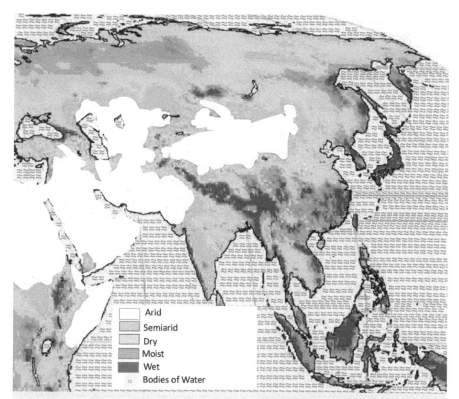

Map 2. The Agro-ecology of Asia. This map is inspired by (but not based exactly upon) the work of Johannes Feddema, 2005. I am grateful to Professor Feddema for his help and encouragement. The map was drawn by William Delgado, Department of Geography, University of Texas, using the Thornthwaite vegetation index

It is firmly oriented to the human use of the environment, whether directly by tillage, or indirectly through domesticated animals such as sheep, horses and camels. Biomass produced by photosynthesis was and is they key limiting factor for both. Biomass potential is determined principally by the combination of temperatures and soil moisture. In the vast northern belt of Eurasia, early frosts and heavy snows precluded crop raising. At the hot arid extreme (shown as white) we would have deserts such as those the historically occupied most of the Arab peninsula, a large part of Inner Asia, much of Iran and northwestern India. Lands suitable for seasonal pasture and at the arid margin for rain-fed farming appear as light gray while moister lands are dark gray. Much of this before and after human use, might be deciduous woodland or thorn-forest savanna. Humid land – which include the classic rice bowls of Asia are shown as black. But as sedentary agriculture needs relatively level ground, much the Himalayan tract extending into Southeast Asia is, in fact unsuitable for this type of agriculture without the investment of much labor in terracing. The map thus (imperfectly, I know) illustrates what limited parts of the continent are in fact suited to the intensive agriculture and dense settlement usually associated with Asia. Instead it shows the large areas where state-building was difficult and populations dispersed. Finally, it shows how much of the Indian subcontinent was in the deciduous forest to savanna continuum when compared with Southeast Asia or China 'within the Wall'.

Dense settlements on fertile lands provided the best basis for the first institutionalization of agrarian hierarchy. Productivity was high, lands and subjects easy to surveil, and taxes easy to extract. Such terrain also created the environmental basis for building social networks and surveillance systems that restrained tax-paying subjects and blocked their escape. Once early states took shape, they could also coercively mobilize large labor forces to clear forests, dig canals, and raise embankments; in short, to radically modify the ecosystem to further empower the new state. James Scott has argued that such states were easiest to construct in riverain alluvial plains where water transport and intensive tillage were both possible.[3] But not all terrain was equally suited for such manipulation, and some areas were adaptable to various lifeways. Resistant peoples and refugees selected these areas. In early imperial China, a popular saying held out the possibility of fleeing south or north to seek refuge among the Yüeh or the Xiong-nu as options open to oppressed commoners.[4] Our map also shows that beyond exceptional regions of the "Fertile Crescent," the great steppe and arid desert extends across most of north-central Eurasia and into north Africa. We therefore begin with its political ecology.

Pastoral Nomadism and "Tribalism"

The conceptual connection between pastoralism and decentralization has nowhere been more salient than in visualizing "tribes." Tribes as social organizations and the characters of their habitats, were conceptually linked by many thinkers down to the present. Ibn Khaldun perceived their natural home to be the open country and especially the seasonally arid deserts. "Those who live by agriculture or animal husbandry cannot avoid the call of the desert, because it alone offers the wide fields, acres, pastures for animals and other things that the settled areas do not offer. It is therefore necessary for them to restrict themselves to the desert." Furthermore, among all pastoralists, he added, it was camel herders who ventured most deeply into the true desert because their beasts thrived on vegetation that other animals could not eat. They also needed the salty water found in the desert. Camel raisers, in his view, were the most savage of all rural peoples, the most given to destructive action in the lands of civilization. But their ability to retreat deep into areas where other men and beasts could not follow allowed them to persist in their role as disruptors of order.[5]

This argument, like the geographical setting it analyzed, was not limited to the western and southern shores of the Mediterranean. The desert extended much further, stretching east to Manchuria and south to peninsular Asia. It contained a great part of Eurasia and was by far the largest tract of pasture available in the Old World. Ibn Khaldun, however, still perceived a lifeway as something shaped by the inescapable necessities of the environment. The only exceptions were affluent townspeople who were shielded from natural forces and human dangers by their wealth and their rulers. But they too were then modified by their environment, becoming effete and cowardly, easy prey for organized nomad bands or turbulent soldiery. Allan Fromherz, the biographer of Ibn Khaldun, found that Khaldun often used "Arab" to mean camel-nomad.[6] Several other ethnonyms such as Shahsevan, Kurd, and Baluch would, in some areas, likewise be understood simply as "tent-dwelling pastoral nomad."[7] Ibn Khaldun also perceived desert tribes as natural founders of kingdoms: he was not surprised that the greatest and not the least tyrannical, of world empires would have been founded by the Mongols, a pastoral people.

Theoretical understanding deepened in the 1930s. It is not coincidental that early theorists were studying the semiarid transition zone between the great seasonal pastures of Inner Asia and the densely settled and intensively tilled lands of Han China. The theory was formulated by Owen Lattimore and Karl Wittfogel. Wittfogel argued that the choice of pastoral life was a deliberate one, not simply an adaptation to the habitat. "After the emergence of stratified agricultural societies," he wrote, free communities faced a serious choice. Shifting to settled agriculture involved accepting the authority of governments and wealthy landowners. This was a deterrent, for under these conditions, a shift might involve submitting to distasteful methods of political and proprietary control. The compromise often was that

> women, children, and war captives tilled some few fields close to a camp site; but the dominant members of the tribe, the adult males, stubbornly refused to abandon their hunting, fishing, or herding activities. The many primitive peoples who endured lean years and even long periods of famine without making the crucial changeover to agriculture demonstrate the immense attraction of nonmaterial values, when increased material security can be attained only at the price of political, economic, and cultural submission.[8]

The historical anthropologist A. M. Khazanov has spent decades in research on this theme. He considers nomadic pastoralism as a form of food production that began with the domestication of animals and plants that marked the human species' entry into the Neolithic Era. Domestication commenced around ten thousand years ago in combination with hunting and gathering. He considers sedentary animal-rearing with free grazing as the most primitive form. Pastoral nomadism was a later specialization. It emerged at various sites and was adopted by elements from both the foraging peoples of the subarctic and the marginal farmers of Neolithic Asia. Seasonally available grasses and shrubs unusable by humans were "harvested" by free-range domesticated animals, especially sheep and horses.

These domesticates were cheaply raised mainly because they lived without fodder stocks, stables, or permanent shelters. They therefore had to be moved with the seasons to find food and escape severe weather. Their human breeders had to adapt to these needs and could not retain more than vestigial elements of fixed habitation. The animals in turn provided transport, meat, milk, hides, and many other products to their keepers. The mix of animals, of course, varied according to habitat and human need. Reindeer were herded near the Arctic, and dromedaries and camels raised in the hot desert core of Asia. But while sheep, goats, cows, horses, and sometimes, camels provided subsistence and transport, the most important animal politically was the horse. It was first domesticated as a food source from a small wild population in Inner Asia. It was then adapted by herdsmen who saw the advantages of guiding and protecting their animals from horseback rather than on foot. But the military advantages it conferred led to its rapid spread across Eurasia (and later, the New World).[9]

Khazanov thus synthesized much research into a description of the minimal social organization of nomadic pastoralism as a food-producing system. This rural lifeway, if undisturbed, did not need complex organization beyond the encampment of a few families who were visited by a handful of artisans and traders. The need for grazing and the seasonal rotation of pastures meant that herding peoples normally had to disperse in small clusters of households. Among the Kazakhs, there were two to four tents in each cluster, rarely as many as eight. There might be an overlay of kinship relations among the tents but "the essence of a nomadic community consists first and foremost in neighbourliness and production."[10] Individuals or groups might break away and move with other clusters. Higher levels of organization might be imposed by outside force or generated by needs of defense. As Lindner perceptively described it, the clan was a nomadic social response to the conditions of a harsh and often insecure life. The larger and more organized tribe was the nomad's "political response to external pressures."[11] Khazanov concurred: he too thought that *internal* requirements for political integration within nomadic societies were too weak to set off a cascading and irreversible process of stratification. It was catalyzed by external pressures, dangers, and opportunities.[12] A centrally imposed pacification in Iran shows how the large tribal aggregations disintegrated once their chieftains lost independent power to withstand the monarchy or coerce the smaller units within their tribe. After a general disarmament in Iran, even small tribes like the Khalfali could deal with the state directly. As one informant told Tapper, a wise elder "said that if we wanted to move freely in our own lands, we must collect and pay our own taxes." They elected their own chief and established direct relations with the regional government. Crucially, paying taxes to the monarchy entitled the tribe to manage its own pastures.[13] But seasonally grazed meadows could not be individually owned either, so in the absence of constraints, social organization devolved down to the level of authority needed for agro-pastoral management, but no further. Maintaining larger political organizations was costly, in terms of time and other resources, for people living in a feast or fast environment. Each camp, however, contained a handful of warriors who, when assembled, became the tribal army. Without a permanent authority structure, concerted tribal action required assembly and deliberation. It therefore required the keepers of many herds and flocks to gather to reach decisions or move off on campaigns. The great nomad encampment was costly and unnecessary in everyday life; indeed, it disrupted the latter. Large herds of grazing and browsing animals could not gather for long. Pasture would be exhausted: disease might spread. But if a ruling elite existed, it could decide and act swiftly. Tribal militarization thus required autocratic leadership. And when it was autocratically mobilized, the self-contained encampment proved its military value. It was only their political needs, offensive and defensive, that periodically united herding camps into tribal armies that, in turn, created conquest empires. Grazing animals could live—*mutatis mutandis*— in many habitats across Asia. It was thus that their flocks and herds that provided the logistical basis of Mongol armies for example. The adaptability of pastoralists to new habitats allowed them to be relocated at the wish of kings and emperors in ways simply impossible for peasant farmers.[14]

The Inner Asian Frontiers of China

The clearest and best documented example of the political shaping of ecological boundaries comes from the Ordos region within the bend of the Yellow River. It was part of a long frontier where lands suited for exploitation by dispersed pastoral encampments shaded into lands also suited for regular tillage. This was the famous—and ever-shifting—"Inner Asian Frontier of China." It was an ecotone, a transitional belt where various forms of land use were possible. It was the balance of power between the pastoralists and the emerging empires of China that determined the patterns of land use and habitation in a wide zone along it.

Chinese historians deemed the Xiong-nu pastoral nomads an ancient presence on the borders of the emerging Chinese civilization. They recorded the construction of long walls to keep them out by several of the "Warring States," beginning as early as 324 BCE. While the walls were represented as defensive, they extended out into lands of grazing and mixed farming in the Ordos region and may also be construed as encroachments by the emerging kingdoms into nomad domain. Its occupation by tax-paying agriculturists, rather than by pastoral farmers with associated tillage, was a result of political pressure. Indeed, Yü reports that "in the First Emperor's time a great number of Chinese had been forced to migrate to the Ordos region to fill the land and guard the frontier. After civil war broke out all of these people fled inland and returned home." This had clearly been an involuntary colonization. Periods when Chinese empires weakened witnessed the return of pastoral nomads to the Ordos plateau once again.[15]

As we have seen, Owen Lattimore, developed the first model of a political ecology of border society in Northeast Asia, and of its relation to sociopolitical life. Nicola Di Cosmo has extended this argument with the addition of much newly uncovered archaeological evidence. Thus the richness of Chinese records has allowed scholars to outline the pattern of political life that developed along the fuzzy frontier dividing lands well-suited to pastoralism and lands well-suited for wheat-millet or, patchily, wet-rice cultivation. In a reconstruction of the earliest farming in the upper Yellow River Basin, Di Cosmo argued that the exploitation of various resources in these borderland regions led to the emergence of mixed farming settlements. Sheep, cattle, and, later, horses were part of the mix of resources, along with grains and other crops.

But hybrid formations were caught between the hammer of the militarized pure nomads moving from Inner Asia and the anvil of an aggressive, centralized agrarian order. They could only survive in periods when neither nomad empires nor Chinese empires were strong. The rise of either forced them into one or the other.

Di Cosmo shows that a sedentary copper- and stone-using culture centered in Kansu (Gansu) extended north and east into Inner Mongolia and the upper Yellow River Valley. It was the most advanced of Chinese cultures in metallurgy. But raising livestock also formed an important part of their subsistence. Their extensive contacts with Inner Asia probably introduced the domestication of the horse and advanced bronze technology into Northern China.[16]

Simultaneously, from 800 BCE onward, several emerging kingdoms of Zhou-era North China pushed into nomad habitat. They sought to dominate or expel the inhabitants and occupy the entire Ordos and beyond. Demonstrating prowess against culturally distinctive peoples (referred to as Jung and Ti) would impress other kingdoms of the Chou ecumene. But these were small populations of farmers and shepherds whose military skills could easily be matched by royal armies. It was their destruction and assimilation, however, that pushed Chinese frontiers onto the borderlands of formidable nomadic horse peoples. The Ordos region in the Yellow River bend, as well as lands north of it, contained wealthy but fully nomadic cultures in the seventh and sixth century BCE. The wealth found in their aristocratic burial sites only increased. By the fourth century BCE, archaeological sites described as "Xiong-nu" contained evidence of luxury trade with the emerging agrarian civilization of China. Graves in the Ordos region now began to evidence considerable new wealth, almost certainly from trade with, service in, and tribute from emerging Chinese kingdoms. The nomads of the Ordos groups created their basic military organization by the early centuries of the Common Era. By then, they were accustomed to combining into confederations under established tribal leaders and could therefore field formidable armies. These appear in the Chinese records as the Xiong-nu.[17]

Lattimore's introduction to the 1951 edition of *Inner Asian Frontiers* generalized this phenomenon to imperial frontier zones generally. Strong empires, he wrote, expanded their power over "barbarian" peoples beyond the frontier. On the other hand, such groups were also driven, by a balance of opportunities and dangers, into hardening their own political organization. Faced with strongly organized opponents, "empires ceased to grow." That was when they could be blackmailed into paying off their borderers. At times, such groups could establish "overlord" regimes over much larger agrarian populations, but that structure would easily disintegrate and revert to a simpler tribal or war-band organization. But the dividing line between the two lands, with their sharply different sociocultural life and subsistence systems, did not run along some hard environmental border: it was rather the result of a long historical process in which different forms of society managed, controlled, and changed their environments. The vast population and tight hierarchy of agrarian China, however, enabled greater and more lasting efforts at reshaping the earth. Nomads, on the other hand, had always moved seasonally. Milder or colder winters, dry or wet weather cycles could be accommodated by modifying their ranges. The vicissitudes of natural conditions might, however, spark fierce competition among nomads if resources shrank overall. Stable stratification and state formation among nomad pastoralists, as Khazanov noted decades ago, has historically speaking, been primarily driven by relations with wealthy sedentary states.[18]

Lattimore and Khazanov's ideas were systematized and further extended by the social anthropologist Thomas Barfield in the 1980s. It was, he argued, necessary to combine anthropology and history to understand the relation of pastoral nomads and sedentary societies over the two thousand years of their interaction. His first question was: "On what basis did the nomads form and maintain states that united regional socio-political organizations?" His book was an effort to answer this question. As he pointed out, the processes that were needed seemed to be a contradiction in terms. How did an autocrat rule large numbers of nomads who still retained their own autonomous organization into lineages, clans, and tribes? This paradox was more acute because economic life was still simple. It was based on small clusters of felt tents whose inhabitants managed livestock within reach of their camps and migrated as the needs of the animals dictated. The economy produced a small and unstable surplus. Droughts or severe winters could destroy much of it in a season.[19] How could authority ever be enforced by the autocrat and his following over an armed, mobile, and constantly dispersible people? The paradox is that the relatively few and poor nomad pastoralists outside the Chinese imperial frontier also periodically threw up a supreme ruler. These kings who ruled over nomadic pastoralists and small oasis settlements could nonetheless mobilize the power necessary to defeat the emperors of the agrarian world. It has been estimated that there were only one million Mongols in China even at the height of the Khubilai's empire around 1260—other parts of the Mongol world empire probably had fewer.[20] But a purely nomad empire would also be chronically short of the resources needed for the enforcement of the Great Khan's will. Permanent troops of retainers could not simply be sustained by their family flocks and dependent labor. They needed loot and pay—preferably both. Raids into and ransoms from agrarian empires might yield all these.

Barfield therefore followed Khazanov in arguing that the origin of steppe empires lay not in the dynamics or needs of pastoral society, but in the tense relationship with adjoining sedentary societies. Not surprisingly, the most formally organized nomadic societies emerged facing China, the world's largest and most centralized sedentary state. Chinese states preceding the Han dynasty had pushed into traditional pastoral lands and expelled or enslaved their inhabitants. But just as wheat, millet, and soybean farming could move northeast beyond the Great Wall, so too could the nomad range be expanded into North China.

Such possibilities drove pastoral peoples to a reactive but also predatory consolidation of their own, and the Xiong-nu nomad kingdom took shape along the frontier of the Han Empire as an ever-present threat that needed to be met with diplomacy, gifts or force. Nomad empires were internally segmented, but their imperial governments monopolized foreign affairs and warfare. Resources extracted from sedentary society funded the imperial center and rewarded the great khan's retainers. They were also shared with tribal segment chiefs and their retainers in the community. Imperial collapse meant a reversion to simpler, autonomous tribal society.

They could do this because the life-skills of the nomadic herdsman and hunter amounted to a form of embodied human capital. It took either long training or birth in the nomad "habitus" to acquire them. The Chinese historian Ssu-ma Chi'en (Sima Qian) described how small Xiong-nu boys were encouraged to ride sheep and shoot small game with bows and arrows. They matured into proficient members of a people who collectively defined themselves as "those who draw the bow." The strength needed to repeatedly draw the nomads' composite bow was built up from early childhood.[21] Once developed, such skills turned an impoverished shepherd youth into a natural cavalryman.

But the nomad shepherd was only one among many peers on the steppe, easy prey for a chieftain's posse. Yet bands of men like him were a menace to even vast numbers of peasant soldiers. It was "the undeveloped division of labor [in pastoral nomad society] that made any pastoralist commoner a mounted warrior where necessary."[22] His family and herds provided the essential logistical basis of his military activity: it was sufficient even for extended campaigns. But it was subject to one major constraint: such self-contained military formations were limited by habitat to areas with adequate year-round grazing for the flocks and herds that moved with the troops.

It was reportedly suggested to the conqueror Khubilai Khan that all the Han be expelled south of the Yangtze and that the north be converted to pure pasture. North China was, in fact, more intensively settled by the Mongols than the lands south of the Yangtze Valley. Consequently, its resident farming population could not recover. Apart from the widespread ravages of the conquest, the Yuan dynasty settled large garrisons with their accompanying herds at key locations. Large areas were allocated to them for grazing. Indeed, about half of North China was the appanage of the Mongol aristocracy. As a result of both the initial massacres, the flight of survivors, and the later conversion of farmland to pasture, the population of the north remained much smaller than the south. North China listed 2 million households in the 1291 census versus 11.4 million in the south. As a result, the north of China was chronically deficient in grain and needed imports from the south to sustain its cities and garrisons. The destruction of southern agriculture might make the continued occupation of the north impossible.[23] The pastoral range could not, in any case, have reached more deeply into south-central China. Humid and hilly terrain would have decimated livestock from the arid steppe. Militarized nomadism could be sustained only in territory suitable for large-scale pastoralism. That, in a sense, served as the ecological limit for nomadic pastoralists to rule as an army of occupation without abandoning their lifeway.[24]

The reverse also applied. The early empires of China soon discovered how the nomads' environment constrained their own armies. Chinese armies moving into the Inner Asian steppe needed to carry their own supplies. A Han era (first century CE) strategist calculated that over 300 days, each soldier consumed eighteen bushels of dried grain. This would be carried by an ox, which would itself need twenty bushels of food. The ox was found to die in a hundred days on expedition. The soldier could not carry even the remaining provisions. But the nomads could scatter into the grasslands with their animals or simply retreat beyond the logistical limit of Chinese power to await the end of the campaigning season. Chinese soldiers also could not bring or presumably gather enough fuel to survive in the bitter late autumn cold. Finally, horses were lost on campaign as well as oxen: even on a victorious campaign under the later Han, less than 30,000 horses returned to China out of 140,000 that had gone out. Recruiting and imitating nomad warriors increased tactical strength. Establishing military farming colonies provided advanced logistical bases that allowed for more extended campaigns, but in the long run, it incurred higher maintenance costs for armies and garrisons.[25]

Active defense nonetheless required such expeditions. Resources needed for the frontier were secured by expanding into "softer" regions, chiefly the far south of China. Empires then undertook vast programs of drainage, irrigation, and town-building that permanently changed the face of the land—initially in North China, but then expanding south across the Yangtze and to the headwaters of the Mekong and Salween. Enormous drainage, flood control, and irrigation projects were built, and great seawalls were maintained to reclaim coastal wetlands for rice cultivation. Vast resources then came from the rice fields, mulberry orchards, and horticulture that replaced lighter forms of subsistence across these lands. Thus, nomad warfare indirectly fed into expanding agrarian settlement. Surpluses were deployed north to protect and defend the steppe frontier of China.

Marked by several walls that culminated in the Great Wall, that frontier hardened. It demarcated the divide between a steppe society of nomadic, militarized "tribes" and one of grain-producing peasants, their literati administrators, and the one emperor who ruled them all. Thus, environmental change and political projects worked together to change the face of the earth across East and Inner Asia. But aggressive advances of increasingly wealthy empires not only forced the nomads to unite for survival. They also generated a long tradition of steppe empires that culminated when Chinggis Khan subordinated all the steppe nomads into one vast confederation. Under his sons and grandsons, it extended its power to the eastern and western edges of Asia and south over China too.[26]

Habitat of Turkic People of Inner Asia

The richness of Chinese records also allows us to look at the west-central parts of Inner Asia. It was dominated for over a millennium by speakers of the Iranian branch of Indo-European languages. They were gradually replaced over a thousand years by speakers of some branch of Turkish. But the numbers of livestock and, consequently, people were limited. The number of pastoralists in Mongolia has been relatively constant from Xiong-nu times to the modern era.[27]

The interaction of pastoralism, farming, and empire was also transformative on the far western edge of Asia. The Mongol Empire seeded Asia with reorganized nomadic peoples as part of its military strategy. Four *tumans*—which at full strength included 40,000 fighting men—were sent to Azerbaijan. Their logistical and productive base moved with them. Rudi Lindner calculates that a total of 200,000 people, accompanied by the equivalent of three to four million sheep, moved onto the pastures of this region. Local Turkic nomads were forced to move. Under the leadership of Osman (1281–1324) and his son, Orkhan (1324–1360), both local tribal warlords, the displaced Turkic nomads began to overrun Byzantine farming communities. The long-settled peasants occupied valleys that were ideal for winter pasture and had shelter for nomadic flocks, which could then quickly move up to summer grazing as the grass grew in spring. Pastoralists displaced arable farmers. Thus, the political impact of distant Mongol activity changed the ecosystem of Anatolia all the way down to the Mediterranean coast. There is no more dramatic example of the working of political ecology than this.

Tribe and Habitat in the Later Ottoman and Iranian World

Lindner has written a valuable history of the emergence of the Ottoman imperial state out of communities of Turkic tribesmen on the western edge of the Mongol Empire. Some had served the Mongols, part of the 40,000 warriors. Others were perhaps displaced or had migrated from fear. Turkic tribesmen, religious warriors, displaced townsmen, and a handful of scribes united under the war chief Osman and his son Orkhan after 1300. That disparate entourage laid the foundation of a great empire, one that even recovered from the ravages of Timur in 1402 and 1403. The Seljuk sultans' victories in Anatolia—farming country hitherto held by the Byzantine Empire—removed that power as a barrier to such movement. Anatolia, like the Ordos Plateau or the Gansu Corridor in China, was land adaptable for either pastoralism or peasant tillage: the Turks decisively shifted it toward pastoralism.

The Byzantine lords had favored populations of subservient peasant farmers. The Turkic chieftains, whose armies came from their nomad followers, tilted in the other direction. Fertile farmland in the valleys could serve as good winter pasture while nearby ridges above 1,000 meters provided grazing and refuge from reprisals. Infiltration and displacement began even before Mongol armies marauded through the area, but it intensified thereafter. The emerging Ottoman Empire, however, gradually developed the tax revenue, military force, and administrative persistence to squeeze out the turbulent Turkish nomads, even though they had been the original basis of Osmanli power before the empire. Some migrated, some were massacred, and many squeezed by administrative power and fiscal demands into settlements. They then merged into farming villages with much reduced flocks and a larger extent of cereal and horticultural production.[28]

The greater Iranian world, from Armenia and Anatolia to Balkh and Baluchistan, was ecologically diverse. But large areas could only be exploited by nomadic pastoralists. Other lands could be tilled, but only with expensive investment in the construction and maintenance of irrigation works. These were often associated with the presence of a dominant lordly class governing a subordinate peasantry whose labor maintained the underground channels that brought snow-melt to arid fields. Water sources, however, were also needed for cattle, sheep, and horses. Outlying fields could provide good grazing for large herds. Just as in Ottoman Anatolia, there was tension between two uses of land and water and two ways of life.

As the Ottoman Empire gradually tightened its grip over nomadic and farming subjects alike, the Turkmen turned to the messianic Safavi movement. Lindner has argued that this movement, in its foundational decades, represented nomads united under a millenarian religious leader. They provided the military basis of the early Safavid sacred kings, who ruled ca. 1500–1722. But while the "natural cavalry of the steppe" could beat back the Uzbeg nomads of Central Asia, they proved incapable of standing against Ottoman infantry and artillery. The Safavid dynasty, therefore, had to develop more regular armies and additionally resorted to leaving a nomad buffer zone as a logistical obstacle to further Ottoman conquest. They encouraged its occupation by pastoral nomads who could inhabit it, but also easily desolate and desert it. Many of the nomads, headed by their chieftains, were enrolled as devotees of the shah and were hence called "Shahsevan." Though they initially were only a band of select disciples, we shall see that this body became a tribal confederacy after the fall of the Safavids. But although the Safavids were a major power in the Iranian lands for two centuries, they could not adopt the Ottoman strategy of sedentarizing nomadic tribes. In part, this was due to the Safavids' dependence on the nomads for military support, but it was also due to the very different environment of the lands the Shahs ruled. Much of that land was inhospitable to peasant villagers and only usable by nomads.

The dynasty collapsed in 1722 before an assault by the Ghilzai tribal insurgents from Afghanistan. A violent interregnum was followed by the emergence of Nadir Shah (r. 1736–47). Though of tribal origin himself, he did not rely on his tribesmen. He instead swept up soldiers united by military discipline and motivated by the abundant plunder he provided them. His rule saw large-scale forced migrations. "His reign left much of Iran, particularly the west, drastically depopulated. Many groups escaped transportation, slaughter and the ravages and requisitions of his campaigns by flight beyond the frontiers or into mountain or desert fastnesses." His regime thus increased the presence of nomadic pastoralists across Iran— and indeed even eastern Iraq—as a consequence of his campaigns there. Later rulers stabilized their own rule by accommodating tribal chiefs, recognizing their headship, and sanctioning their control of the allotment of pastures among encampments and families. Tapper describes how tribal organization might either persist or decay into a "normal" landlord-tenant relationship. The latter might occur when impoverished herdsmen, their herds destroyed by some calamity and were then forced into other forms of subsistence. It might also occur when a whole tribe under its chief moved toward farming after securing title to land, now guaranteed by the increasingly powerful monarchy. Meanwhile, the Russian Empire, and later, the Soviet Union, shut many nomads out of their best pastures. The stabilization of the Qajar dynasty also gradually eroded tribal power and encouraged settlement into villages. The final blow came under the new (Pahlavi) dynasty founded by Reza Shah in the 1920s.[29]

Community Organization and Habitat in South Asia

East of the Iranian lands lies the ecologically and culturally diverse Indian subcontinent, or South Asia. The social anthropologist Fredrik Barth arrived there a few years after Leach and was deeply influenced by him. Barth developed a model of ethnic partitioning by studying the Swat Valley and the adjoining uplands at the eastern edge of Afghanistan. This is a fertile enclave of intensive agriculture in today's northwest Pakistan. The lower valley could grow two crops, including rice. The upper valley was colder and more rugged. Yields were lower, surpluses precarious. Barth studied the area in the 1950s and developed a persuasive model of its political ecology.[30]

Barth drew upon the analytic models pioneered by Lattimore and Leach and provided an important description of ecological and cultural boundaries in a fertile, irrigated valley in the mountains of 1950s Pakistan. The valley had been conquered by an alliance of Yusufzai chiefs and their followers in the sixteenth century. But even though the Yusufzai were capable of conquering all the cultivable lands, Barth observed a tacit boundary beyond which they did not expand. That boundary, between the Yusufzai Pathan tribe living as a minority of dominant lords—or at least substantial farmers—and Kohistani subsistence farmers, lay along the line where surplus-yielding agriculture ceased to be possible. The dominant Yusufzai had cultural norms that required the presence of subordinates. Subsistence hill farmers could not afford to maintain dependents. The militarily weaker Kohistanis were therefore left undisturbed in the poorer territory even though they were unable to defend it. Its low productivity would not sustain the lordly style that the Yusufzai had developed as a tribal cultural marker. Finally, a community of Gujar herdsmen exploited interstitial grazing resources that became seasonally available in summer and fall. These pastures could only be used by herdsmen who were prepared to follow their herds over a wide circuit, which the Yusufzai thought was degrading. Barth divided the Gujars into true nomads and seasonally transhumant graziers.[31] Thus, three distinct communities had niches in a given ecosystem. But one of them, the Yusufzai landlords, developed from a conquest tribe into what social anthropologists term a dominant caste. I have argued that this pattern also existed elsewhere in South Asia.

The Indian subcontinent was generally more arid and more deeply intersected with woodland than agrarian China (meaning the lands within the Great Wall). On the other hand, it was neither as rugged, nor as moist or forested, as most of Southeast Asia. Its northwestern portion was effectively an extension of the West Asian semiarid zone. Further east, though humid forest and delta were also found. South Asia therefore had a mosaic of farming and pastoral regions. States here were more fragile and more centrifugal than in East Asia. Empires were generally short-lived. South Asia was also characterized by strong community organizations and had been so from early historic times. But the agrarian potential of the region had led to a "layering" of tribal organization across the landscape wherever a reliable agrarian surplus allowed it. Deeper soils and moister climates also allowed various types of woodland to exist in the center and east. These ranged from thorn scrub to dense deciduous forests or even rain forests. Classical Indian texts warned kings of many dangers. One class of turbulent folk were described as forest dwellers—*atavika*. As peasant farming expanded into the woodlands of North and Northeast India, it would not be surprising if forest-dwellers took to raiding and foraging among settled agriculturists. Even the pacifist Buddhist emperor Ashoka (r. ca. 270–238 BCE) advised them to preserve their lives by not transgressing against his empire. Abandoned farmland reverted to forest or formed a savanna-forest ecotone. Almost two thousand years later, a Maratha official reviewing the situation in Central India around 1813 wrote, "There are many trees in this province, therefore the peasants are troubled by tigers and robbers, and human settlement cannot grow. Hence the revenue officers should be instructed to cut down trees within their districts and increase settlements."[32]

South Asian agriculture overall was therefore more diverse than in the classic rice bowls of East Asia. Much of the land could sustain several alternative lifeways, from foraging and grazing through shifting agricultureto permanent tillage. Farmers often supplemented their diet with wild foods and game. They were often quite mobile. All classes in the region made strategic use of woodlands and even promoted their growth.

The Turkic warrior Babur began his raids in North India and Eastern Afghanistan in the early sixteenth century before finally conquering the sultans of Delhi and founding the future Mughal Empire. In a political survey of the country he had conquered, Babur observed that there were seven majorkings: five Muslims and two "infidels." But he also added that "the mountains and jungles are held by many petty rays and rajahs." Smaller domains were evidently protected by the terrain they inhabited. Babur also observed what were clearly peasant responses to political and climatic distress. One was resistance, the other mobility. Houses were walled and roofed with grass and wood. Unlike the lands of Inner Asia with which Babur was familiar, crops were usually rain-fed and so needed no irrigation. At most, a settlement needed a well or pond for drinking, and one could be dug quickly if needed. If they were overtaxed or frequently robbed, peasants voted with their feet. A village or town, Babur wrote with some exaggeration, would be quickly built or abandoned in a day or a day and a half.[33] Heavily grazed, or farmed and then abandoned, lands would soon be spontaneously covered with thorny forest and scrub. Even foot soldiers would move with difficulty, and horsemen would be scattered and risk injury to their expensive mounts. It was not coincidental that Babur noted the presence of thickets of thorn brush in the plains of North India. Peasants defended by these would resist the demands of marauding tax collectors.

The thorn woodland was thus a precipitate of political processes—a resource for some, an obstacle for others. Once established, it might be persistent. In 1851, a British survey officer wrote:

> On entering the Province [Khandesh, North Maharashtra] from almost any quarter, the face of the country appears to be covered with low, scattered bush jungle. This jungle is composed of various kinds of thorny bushes, of which the 'Bear' with its recurved thorns is the most abundant. These bushes are seldom more than 10 feet in height and usually much less. They do not generally grow very close together, but here and there dense and almost impervious thickets are met with . . . in a year or two, after a field so cultivated is relinquished, the jungle has grown as thick as ever and there is nothing to indicate that the field has ever been under tillage at all.[34]

A Tribe of the Thorn Forest: Bhils of Central India

The case of the Bhil "tribes" of Central India demonstrates how political and economic relations were embedded in and also generated a particular environment. In this case, it was the tangled secondary forest that occupied much of northern Maharashtra. The Bhils supplemented swidden farming with hunting and gathering. Their weapons were locally made bows and arrows. Their familiarity with the terrain made them formidable in their own woodlands, and they were aware that the forest was their stronghold. Living in small independent clusters of houses and moving to new sites from time to time meant that they developed initiative and valued autonomy. John Malcolm was an experienced colonial official who had often negotiated with Bhil chiefs. He wrote in 1827 that there was a "natural spirit of independence in the mountain Bhills, which compels Chiefs who have a desire to establish an authority that supersedes that of the *Tarwis* [headmen] of small colonies to entertain followers from a distant country. . . . *Their arms, and their habits are more suited to the ravines, the woods and the mountains amid which they live.*"

Outsiders visiting the forests were also prone to severe, often fatal, attacks of fever, probably malaria. Maratha soldiers posted to remote jungle outposts before colonial rule suffered too. To give one example: the commandant of Kukarmunda, Janardhan Raghunath Sukhatme, sent Tipu Khan and his men to the outposts of Valheri and Kolvi. But, the writer continues, the air was bad, the water did not suit them, they all fell ill, and "the Bhils carried them back to the fort on cots. Some died, the rest were medicated and cured, and men from the fort garrison were sent to hold the posts. But the air does not suit them, they fall ill, therefore Tipu Khan's men refuse to go to the outposts and no one from the other units is prepared to go either." The Bhils, it will be noted, were unaffected by the malarial fever.

The British were to have the same experience a few years later. Of five officers who proceeded during August to the Mangrode jungles, "three died within a fortnight of their return; and few descend to the Dang at any season of the year without suffering from fever. During a short campaign of three months, of five officers one died and three left India on sick certificate; and of three hundred [Indian] regulars who were employed, [only] one hundred and twenty marched back to Malligaum."

In times of political turmoil, such as the era that preceded British rule, Bhil chiefs retreated into the hill forests and attempted to exercise suzerainty by plunder. But this was a prelude to asserting various claims before whatever authority might succeed in controlling the plains. Following the defeat of the Nizam-ul-mulk at Bhopal in 1738, this was clearly the Peshwa, and as early as 1740, some unidentified Khandesh Bhils presented themselves before him and stated that they had hereditary claims to specified amounts of cash, grain, sugar, cloth, and other materials from the villages. Dues for these goods, however, were not being paid at present, so they petitioned for their restoration. Letters were duly issued to the local officials of eight Khandesh subdivisions to pay these dues in conformity with local custom. This was part of a pattern of negotiation and revenue sharing that was needed to ensure local tranquility that would allow agriculture and the taxes and tributes that it yielded.

After 1818, colonial rule brought a more sustained, and militarily more powerful, effort to subdue and control the peoples of the woodlands. Elphinstone wrote in 1822:

> The plan adopted . . . was to stop the supplies of the Beels, which are all drawn from the plain; to cut off any parties that attempted to issue to plunder, and to make vigorous attacks on the points in the hills, to which the principal Beel Chiefs had retired. These measures soon reduced the Beels to accept the very favorable terms held out to them; which were to forbear their depredations, the Chiefs receiving pensions, and allowances for a certain number of men, and binding themselves to restrain the excesses of their people.

John Malcolm in Malwa (now part of the Indian state of Madhya Pradesh), made similar arrangements for the hill peoples. He described it as "giving them their ancient dues, encouraging cultivation in their Hills, instituting markets for their wood, etc., and raising a Bheel Corps composed of the most barbarous of the class and commanded by their own Chiefs."

The British government was, however, more persistent than any Indian regime had been: it also possessed greater superiority in armament, surveillance, and communication. Tribal chiefs of all kinds were induced to submit by pension and land grants. They may have become more oppressive as their ability to exact tribute from peasant society shrank. As early as 1824, the officer appointed to "pacify" the Bhil population reported that these chiefs had all hired foreign mercenaries. The "endless petty exactions and haughtiness of these armed miscreants," he wrote, kept the Bhils poor and led them to seek help from the British officers. That obviously weakened the Bhils and provided information to the colonial government. Meanwhile, recalcitrant chiefs and their followers were hunted down.

It was not until the middle decades of the nineteenth century that the British imperial regime was finally able to put in place the policies that were to lead inexorably to a steady thinning of the forests and a sedentarization of their inhabitants. In effect, this gradually reduced the kings of the forest to the serfs of the forest department that needed labor for its timber operations. Many residents were expelled, fire farming (swidden) was forbidden, and residents of forest areas were compelled to work on Forest Department projects. The erosion of the forests and a rising agrarian population began to encroach on Bhil territory. The peasant population increased and pushed back woodlands, field by field. Beginning in the 1850s, railways began to cross the Indian subcontinent and burn prodigious amounts of wood fuel. They also transported timber and forest produce. Deprived of leadership, and increasingly unable to find refuge in the forests, ordinary tribal folk began to work seasonally in others' fields or cut, gather, and sell forest products. Moneylenders flourished as never before, sometimes combining their trade with making and selling liquor. Tribal chiefs became pensioners of the British and tribal solidarity was lost. The Bhil "tribe" survived only as a category of colonial ethnography and postcolonial politics. [35]

Southeast Asian Examples of Political Ecology

The Southeast Asian Massif—a region of high mountains, swift-flowing rivers, and often dense forest—extends from South China, west through Vietnam, to Burma, and into large parts of Eastern India and Bangladesh. The most important—indeed trailblazing—study of the interaction of lifeway and terrain was made by Edmund Leach in northern Burma. This region was a mosaic of communities—seemingly culturally and linguistically distinct—that were spread across the deeply dissected landscape. These were small hill communities that periodically shifted village sites to find fresh forest land for swidden (earlier pejoratively called 'slash and burn'), as well as larger settlements with a wider range of subsistence under a chieftain. Finally, there were valley floor rice growers in hierarchical societies under small kings who were often subordinate to a central imperial figure. Those in the latter category, who grew "wet" rice in seasonally flooded paddy fields and were Buddhists, were identified ethnically as "Shan." [36] Generations of earlier scholars had sought to classify the hill farmers of rain-fed crops as "primitive," "semi-civilized," and "civilized." Quite often, they also classified them along racial lines and suggested waves of immigration and conquest that had pushed "primitive" communities out of the best lands. They had, it was suggested, retreated into remote upland refuges where they practiced primitive swidden agriculture supplemented by hunting. Here, habitat reflected relative power and the process of conquest. Leach overturned this theory by arguing that the distribution of ethnic performance and settlement reflected political and social choices, albeit with a historical time lag.

In Leach's analysis, the peoples most detached from hierarchy and external power were the *gumsa* communities. They lived in little autonomous clusters of houses—often less than ten. They gathered wild foods, hunted, and cultivated *taungya* or swidden fields, moving as necessary. But a larger population on a similar subsistence base could form a *gumlao* community, part of a structured hierarchy of authority up to the "great domain chief." The latter's authority might reach down slope to the valley floor. But the expensively built, carefully managed rice fields of the lower levels were inhabited by people called Shan. These communities were village-centered, often locally endogamous and focused around wet-rice tillage. They were controlled by local princes. Leach analytically divided the region into three zones.

> **Zone A:** more or less prosperous *taungya* with the possibility of either *gumsa* or *gumlao*.

> **Zone B:** grassland *taungya* with crop rotation in the hills and wet rice in the valleys; all political organization was of the *gumsa* type. Cooperation between valley wet-rice growers and hill villages was essential to this mode of subsistence. The Shan could pressure Kachin communities of this type by cutting off their access to valley floors.

> **Zone C:** steeper hillsides, grassland and forest *taungya*, but terracing where fixed villages have to be maintained. Leach argued that fixity was due to military concerns and/or to maintain the lucrative control of hill passes through which taxable commodities to and from South China traveled.

Leach consistently emphasized that differences in physical environment produce only a partial explanation of differences in political or cultural organization. He also argued that individuals and families often made the transition between the two forms of sociocultural life. "But this kind of thing was anathema to the tidy bureaucratic minds of British officials." Down to the very end of their rule, they sought to mark out precise boundaries between Shan and Kachin because they were classed as separate racial elements.[37]

A generation later, James Scott particularly valorized the small anarchic hill communities as examples of successful evasion of the state. He especially emphasized the environmental features of their management of the habitat. He began by laying out a stylized model of the flooded rice-growing or "padi state." This needed water management, coordinated planting, and legible landscape susceptible to—indeed requiring control by—superior authorities. It concentrated population and produced large surpluses to support an overlord class. On the other hand, there were landscapes and production methods that were resistant to monitoring and subordination. Scott saw the New World food crop—cassava or tapioca—as characteristically suited to such social regimes. Not surprisingly, it spread rapidly in the mountain massif of Southeast Asia. It did not need careful preparation or collective water management. Nor could it be found, measured, or taxed as easily as rice in the field or the granary. It was therefore well adapted to resistance and evasion. Peoples in the Zomia lands, Scott added (following Leach and F. K. Lehman), changed their social structures depending on their relationship to imperial powers in their vicinity.[38] A similar assessment of political relationships affecting cropping and residence is offered by the anthropologist Jean Michaud. Many strains of rice were evolved and cultivated in different ways. If hill slopes were relatively gentle and peasant labor could be controlled in a form of feudalism, then extensive terraces were carved into the hills with "wet" rice being cultivated. But where peoples were still mobile and land was not secure as property, unirrigated or "dry" rice was raised in rain-fed swidden fields. "This is the dominant form of rice production among lineage societies in the massif."[39]

The Political Ecology of Tribal Life: Conclusion

To sum up, then, "tribes" have existed and continue to exist across politically and ecologically varied lands. It was their "ungovernability," not their mode of production, that determined their sociological label. Some landscapes, some lifeways, were more resistant to external mapping and control: some were indeed modified for precisely that purpose.

On the borders of the great steppes and in their semiarid extensions in West Asia, "tribal" people were conceived as pastoral nomads. But they might also be settled peasants with traditions of tribal solidarity governed by their own chiefs. Tapper writes of the overlap in the Iranian world, where great cities and rich farmlands were scattered like islands in the sea of rugged deserts and arid pastures. The latter were the territory of nomads. Nomads, by virtue of their shifting residences, and tribespeople, because of their allegiances to each other or to their chiefs, were always difficult to control. These entities were therefore mentally assimilated with one another: the tribe was perceived as the characteristic organization of nomads but one that could be found elsewhere too.

Tribes existed as a mosaic of ungovernable communities across Afghanistan from which several ruling elites emerged in the eighteenth century. Historical sociologists have often noted that tenaciously persistent kinship systems depend on collective institutions, such as property, and are more characteristic of landed families than any other group. In the same way, strong and persistent "tribal" organization paradoxically existed in the Swat Valley, where the tribe collectively ruled other communities and developed collective structures of action to exclude both the market and the king.

But in the narrower and more dissected lands of the Hindukush, extending into the western edges of the Indus Basin, many tribes were pugnacious settled cultivators, with irrigation works, orchards, and gardens. Further east, in the varying but semiarid to moist deciduous lands of South Asia, "tribals" were again specialized users of the woodlands relying on them for subsistence, for defense, and for predation. But like the Thakurs of Bareilly, they could also become a dominant stratum of turbulent farmers and small landlords. In the humid and rugged Southeast Asian Massif, they were ever-shifting swidden cultivators perched on inaccessible hilltops, ever-ready to raid and vanish. They were therefore also valuable militiamen, repeatedly drawn into the politics of kingdoms and empires.

This chapter has thus outlined the many habitats where tribes existed before the twentieth century. These all had some key political characteristic: they were resistant to centralized authority that might subject their peoples to the hard and humiliating life of ordinary peasants. The basis of that recalcitrance might be natural conditions in a broad sense: arid lands, high mountains, dense thickets. But all these, I have argued, were not entirely given features of the terrain. They were managed environments, controlled as sites of defense and offense. Lifeways were adapted to the optimal utilization of such natural features that gave tribal folk a strategic advantage. The "pure" pastoral life of Mongolia and Turkestan; the small clusters of houses hidden on a high ridgetop; thorn thickets used and protected in many parts of Asia—all represented a dynamic adaptation to the human geography where tribal communities survived. Such interaction of ecology and power is the crux of "political ecology," of the adaptation of habitat and political organization to values and conduct and vice versa.

4

TRIBES, YESTERDAY AND TODAY

"The tribal peoples ... do not retain their tribal institutions through ignorance, but as a stable and successful adaptation to the natural and social environment in which they find themselves."
— Fredrik Barth, 1962

Introduction: The Purpose of This Chapter

I have, up to this point, ranged widely across Asia (and often beyond) in order to draw out specific themes and arguments. Chapters 1 and 2 worked out the relation between words and things in the East and the West respectively. Chapter 3 explained the relation between "tribe" as a political organization and the ecological setting that it inhabited and produced.

My introduction to this book began, however, with an argument about the contemporary world. I have already argued that "tribe" can be *at once* a lazy-minded external label, an internalized self-description, a "habitus," and a type of political life. In many parts of the world, it is now also an administrative label applied to many different entities. As a historian, I would say that above all, the "tribe" is type of political organization created in reaction to the threat from other tribes or from centralized states, typically kingdoms. It is, therefore, no more permanent than a kingdom and an empire, than a one-party state or a national republic. It may dissolve and reform, just as these other entities do, as the larger world around them changes. Imperial states like the Mongols could hammer tribes into new military formations that disregarded older ethnic boundaries. But when empires fell, fragments, if they landed in suitable habitats, hardened into tribes anew.

These are large and abstract arguments. This chapter, therefore, offers the reader a series of case studies of individual tribes in their historical trajectory to the present. In the twentieth century, these tribes sometimes dissolved entirely into new national states, sometimes survived as socio-political organizations like castes, and sometimes were reborn as new, armed, and autonomous tribes. It will thus concretely illustrate arguments already made, and connect them to the present.

Northern Asia: Manufactory of the Peoples

Northern Asia—or roughly the geographical regions of Siberia, Manchuria, Inner and Outer Mongolia, former Soviet Central Asia, the Don-Volga steppe and Tibet—forms the largest portion of the Asian landmass. But this portion has also historically been the most thinly populated. Yet the Romans, seeing it from its far western edge, called it the "manufactory of the peoples and womb of nations." There seemed be an unending array of new peoples emerging from the East. The paradox is that this "manufactory" actually had a comparatively small population, but its peoples and languages were mutable and unstable, not anchored to lands and lords and priests like the vast peasant populations of the agrarian empires around their margins. The confusion of victory and defeat, of fragmentation, migration, and flight over vast distances, meant that ethnogenesis was constant and ongoing.

Many important examples of empire-building tribes were peoples of pastoral nomadic heritage. The previously noted historical association of nomad pastoralists with "tribal" organization reflects the necessary characteristics of their life across the immense geographical expanse from Korea to Poland, from the Sea of Japan to the Black Sea.

Not all empire-building tribes were steppe pastoralists. The Manchus were only the last of the imperial powers to emerge out of the steppe-to-forest transition zone of Northeast Asia. Whatever their origin, tribes constantly emerged as secondary organizations around the margins of wealthy agrarian states. Steppe pastoralists, as I have already argued, were preadapted to become nomadic empires. In nomad home territory, they had to draw on external sources of tribute and plunder so as to subsidize the professional warrior bands that enforced the will of great Khans. In default of that resource, they broke apart into tribes of a few thousand, or yet smaller, bands. Steppe empires were shaped by exceptional leaders who mobilized the nomads to plunder and conquest.

Inner Asian empires based entirely on nomad warriors could thus disintegrate back into the tribes from which they emerged. An ongoing tributary relationship with stabler agrarian systems—notably that of China—would harden tribal warriors into a ruling elite. External resources would stabilize the consumption of that crucial military elite. Ethnically distinct garrison centers would gradually shift the relationship away from plunder and toward taxation. Conquerors who founded empires in the agrarian zone could be socially dissolved by the process of running the governments they established. If they persistently retained a separate nomad warrior identity, they would encyst in the body of an agrarian society. That would carry the risk of being expelled by the host if they weakened, which is what happened to the Yuan dynasty that the Mongols established in China.

At the southeastern edges of the great sea of grass, where nomads ruled supreme, lay East Asia, and pastoral salients entered its agricultural zone through the Gansu Corridor and Ordos Plateau. This transitional region witnessed the most audacious, yet in many ways the most tenacious, success of social engineering found in Eurasia. Chinese imperial regimes learned from each successive phase of nomad conquest, especially that of the Mongols. The last Chinese empire, the Qing, had not emerged from a nomadic tribal conquest. They instead laid claim to the heritage of the Jin empire of Northeast China. The founders, however, sought to create a Manchu military ethnos "*as though*" there had been a conquest tribe that founded their empire. They followed the Mongol pattern of maintaining numerous garrisons of ethnically distinct troops with allotted estates for their support. But they consciously sought to develop and propagate a set of practices that would solidify the Manchu tribal identity and supposed martial character.[1]

The Qing also continued the long Han drive to conquer the southeast, a habitat suited to the rice-farming habitus characteristic of that civilization. This conquest went through several stages, and early Han immigrants like the Hakka had sometimes acculturated to the local communities in phases of imperial weakness. But the push was resumed by the 1680s and continues to the present.

With the exception of Vietnam, however, kings beyond the effective imperial Chinese boundary aspired to be Buddhist universal monarchs on the Indic model. In practice, as S. J. Tambiah suggested, they developed a "galactic polity"—autocratic in the rice lands of the valleys and omnipotent in a sacred and royal center, but weakly connected to the hard-to-rule, unprofitable hilltops and ravine-riven hillsides. The latter are the 'Zomia' lands already mentioned in earlier chapters.

South Asia is discussed in the last part of this chapter. Ecologically and politically, it forms a transition zone eastward from the desert pastures of Inner Asia, the rugged mountains of the Hindu Kush, and west of the great valleys and rain forest of Southwest China and Southeast Asia. State forms resembling both the galactic polities of Southeast Asia and the nomad conquest states of Inner Asia appeared in South Asia. In this region, tribes were "enclaved," either occupationally or geographically, within state societies that encrusted them. This formation was characteristic of South Asia. Conquerors might invent themselves as a conquest tribe presiding over a caste system or as a smaller lordly elite in a peasant society. They might also live on the margin of an agrarian society as bellicose claimants to tribute and aspirants to kingship—by aspiration, not noble savages but savage nobles. They might also fit into extant hierarchies through special habitation or profession, whether as hunters and watchmen, armed merchants, or seasonally migrant shepherds.

Thus, looking over Asia, we would see that a spectrum of organizations persisted across the centuries, especially where the landscape was best utilized by seasonally nomadic folk. They might exist as pastoralists across the sea of seasonal grazing that surrounded islands of tillage, whether in oases or favored valleys and deltas. Modern states have been intrinsically hostile to mobile peoples, especially to those who roamed across international boundaries. From the eighteenth century onward, states were organizations of settled people that settled people. But the great "settling down" or sedentarization of the world gradually squeezed nomads, whether organized in tribes, castes, or bands, into the farming economy, the industrial economy, and sometimes, the illicit drug economy. The strength of dominant states and the character of the regional ecosystem provided the frame for this.

In some densely peopled settings, we shall see formerly nomadic herdsmen might grow into great bands of militant caravan traders like the Banjaras in South Asia. They might alternatively, like the Rohillas who will be considered below, develop into a regional landlord elite that also supplied the market for mercenary soldiers. They might form a nomadic segment of peasant society, exploiting seasonal resources and supplementing peasant farming as they traveled seasonally from autumn settlement to summer pasture. Or they might form a closed nomadic community offering services to but also preying upon settled village society. By the mid-nineteenth century, these last were under British colonial surveillance. In some cases, they were reduced to occupying a caste niche in the vast honeycomb of South Asian society, though they might not be called a "caste," but a "tribe." The cases presented in this chapter will concretize these arguments.

Turkic Peoples

The implosion of the linguistically Indo-European empires of Inner Asia after 500 CE was followed by the emergence and expansion of Turkic-speaking peoples across the same region. Having acquired a horse culture, they quickly founded a conquest empire. It did not endure. But fragments of the Turkic peoples generated enduring new tribes and ethnicities across the region from Xinjiang to Bosnia, often replacing languages and absorbing peoples.

Tribes that remained on the steppe, but who became immobile around permanent sites, constantly risked destruction by other, hungrier nomads. This is what happened to the great Uygur empire soon after 800 CE. At that time, it dominated Inner Asia and extracted vast tributes from the Tang whom it sporadically protected against the Tibetans and internal rebellions. Their capital was strategically located deep in Central Asia, almost impossible for Tang armies to attack. Its great Qagans built up an imperial center surrounded by farming settlements and frequented by long-distance traders. But increasing inequality within the Uygur "manifested in the growing sedentarization of the elite and the loss, as the Chinese sources point out, of 'barbarian' virtues, was an important element in the internal strife." Furthermore, tied down to their immensely wealthy capital, the Uygur emperors "had lost the single most important military advantage nomads possess: mobility." Meanwhile, their capacity for war was weakened by epizootics and epidemics. Animal deaths in exceptionally severe weather worsened the crisis, and bitter internal conflicts exposed their vulnerability. Their capital was sacked and destroyed by the Kirghyz nomads whom the Uygurs had once dominated and oppressed. The remains of the once imperial community fragmented into the steppe pastoral tribes from which it had but recently emerged.[2]

The Turks of Western Eurasia

Four centuries later, the Mongols appeared from the steppe margins. Expanding swiftly, they ranged west as far as the shores of the Mediterranean, driving some communities before them, subjugating others, and making and planting novel groups across their domains according to political need and military accident. Out of this maelstrom between 1200 and 1400 CE, there emerged a West Asian tribal people whose conquests and state-building radically transformed the eastern Mediterranean world with effects that last to the present. These were the Ottoman Turks.

Rudi Lindner succinctly describes the social structures necessitated by their way of life a thousand years ago. Herders had to cooperate to manage and protect their animals. Cooperation and self-protection required temporary congregation in camps and the recognition of lineages "real or fictitious." Clans might be grouped into tribes by the choice to follow an effective chief or a powerful conqueror. Genealogical inconsistency or fabrication was needed to provide the necessary flexibility to adapt to the ever-changing circumstances of the nomad's world. Around 1300, Osman and his son Orkhan began to gather a following in Anatolia. Turkic pastoral nomads had been migrating to the region for two centuries. The Mongols added four *tumans*—40,000 warriors (if at full nominal strength)—to the area. This meant the addition of perhaps 200,000 people and millions of grazing animals to the area. Grazing land was scarce and village fields were unprotected by any force capable of withstanding the Turkic nomads. Peasant farmers—typically Greeks—were gradually ousted from many areas.

It was in the aftermath of these upheavals that Osman began building up a tribal kingdom on the edges of the retreating Byzantine power while the Mongols were preoccupied by their own conflicts. "Osman's first success as a tribal chief was due to his ability to protect the few, strong common interests of his tribesmen: pasture, the hunt, and survival." He successfully "served as a fulcrum between tribal and external interests."[3] Once the house of Osman achieved some stable power, it needed to change its structure to operate within a more complex political system. In the new system, the tribesmen were not the sole, or even the most important, fellow tribesmen of a chief: they had to be transformed into "a few of the many subjects of a sultan." New artillerymen and full-time slave soldiers emerged as the core of the new Ottoman state. Tax-paying farmers and skilled artisans were needed to sustain it. And merchants, moving safely across sea and land, carried the many necessities and luxuries that the new system needed. Autonomous bands of free-range warrior shepherds were an enduring threat. Their chiefs were often included in the Ottoman landed classes. Meanwhile, impoverished nomads were gradually excluded from military roles and pushed into farming society. The Ottoman dynasty was enduringly changing their world and dissolving the remaining Turkic nomads into minor components of a grand imperial system.[4]

The Making of Mongols and the Reshaping of Eurasia

I have already introduced the most famous of all tribal nomads: the Mongols. Neither the ethnic name "Mongol" nor the tribe itself were ancient. Three experts on the long history of Inner Asia have analyzed the Mongols as the culmination of a long tradition of nomadic empires going back to the emergence of the Xiongnu after 300 BCE. A key element of the tradition was the recognition of a ruling clan over all the tribes. If we look at it functionally, the general acceptance of such a concept canalized centralization by reducing the number of potential claimants. The dominant clan came to power and demonstrated its charisma by victorious conquest. In that sense, it was tested by the duration of its career of success: so was each claimant to its leadership.

Successive formations of this kind had risen and fallen in the millennium preceding the rise of Chinggis around 1200 CE. His was a military aristocratic state. It emerged after a long period of internal wars that "transformed traditional group identities and continued to manipulate them."[5] It was perhaps observation of such processes that had led the eleventh-century Han savant Ouyang Xiu to declare that the nomadic barbarians indeed had tribes and leaders, but could not have *real* lineages because they had no good genealogical records. Functionally, however, instability would actually be a source of strength and flexibility. Ancestry could be reworked, and corporate identity could be adjusted to the needs of the time. The better documented and, therefore, inflexible Chinese lineages never became anything more than local defense associations in times of great disorder.[6]

The Mongols certainly oversaw a vast ethnic re-ordering on a grand scale in pursuit of a universal empire ruled by Chinggis and his descendants. Peter Golden writes that the core of the tribe originated on the forest edge of the steppe in South Siberia and Eastern Mongolia. The very name "Mongol" was little known before the twelfth century.[7] But the adaptation to pastoralism and horse warfare transformed them.[8] Chinggis operated adroitly in a world whose basic components were loosely structured tribes (*irgen*), or often merely the clan, or *obogh*.[9] During the imperial phase, civilian populations, especially craftsmen and engineers, were conscripted and resettled like warriors, to suit the political and military needs of their overlords.

Thus, the political redefinition of stable units of collective life reached a high point under the Mongol Empire. But it was also an unsustainable apogee, and when the structure fell apart, its fragments were distributed across Asia. As Barfield observes, the ideal of a self-sustaining hereditary army was an old steppe tradition, effective in its own environment. But it was hard to transplant. Nomad troops were expected to need no training and to provide their own weapons and logistics. But once garrisoned in (for example) China, it was far more difficult to maintain such a tradition. Allotted lands and slaves proved insufficient to sustainably support a soldiery whose men were long absent on distant frontiers. Even by the 1350s, Mongol garrisons had lost their effectiveness and could not cope with Chinese rebels unaided.[10] Subsequently, if left to fend for themselves in pastoral habitats, they reconstituted themselves into loose aggregations of tent-clusters. These renascent tribes were often constituted on the basis of genealogical linkage with some past ruler or ancestor, legendary or historical.

Lineages would therefore be scattered and re-sorted into new tribes united by the needs of nomadic subsistence and defense as well as the opportunities of conquest and plunder. Atwood has described this in "Banner, Otog, Thousand." He argued "that pre-modern Mongolian society did indeed have a basic unit in a system of territorial divisions." These he termed "appanage communities." They went on to provide the structure of Mongol political organization into the twentieth century. Atwood writes that "the Mongols, wherever documented, have been organized into what we can call appanage communities, usually numbering from the several hundred to several thousand households in size, and which show considerable continuity (on the order of one or two centuries)." Documentation, as I have already argued, arises in budding states. Gellner in 1984 already pointed to the fact that a 'feudal' model of the Mongols derives its evidence from times when they were either conquering (the Chinggisid age) or conquered (the Manchu imperial era).[11]

Under Chinggis and his immediate successors, the largest organizations were usually known as the *ulus*, ruled by a particular subordinate Khan or ruler. The empire founded by Chinggis, however, broke up into feuding domains by 1400. Fragments of the peoples who had been swept up in the whirlwind were deposited in various parts of Asia. Defeat could lead to bands of survivors heading in different directions. Those who were pastoral nomads at the outset, and who retained some basis in the livestock economy, could return to that life in a new setting. But survival in the hard conditions of Inner Asia during the Iron Age required submission to a military and political leadership capable of mobilizing significant force as necessary. Scattered pastoral encampments would not survive long.

The Mongol (Yuan) dynasty was forced to evacuate China in the 1360s under pressure from peasant rebels and their own fissions. The remains of the Mongols persisted as a threatening presence beyond the border of the Ming Empire. The Manchu rulers of the Qing dynasty, who replaced the Ming in the 1640s, were deeply aware of the Mongol presence and sought systematically to enfeeble them as a political alternative by "feudalizing" Mongol social structure. "Banners" were created among the Mongols on extant Qing patterns in the 1680s. They followed new administrative lines whose divisions mimicked those of the Eight Banners. "The restructuring of Khalkha Mongolia demanded not only the creation of new jurisdictions but also the integration of the noble class of the steppe, through the usual means of marriage alliances and incorporation of the steppe leaders into the imperial aristocracy."[12]

From Turkman Messianic Entourage to Iranian Empire and Back

Many Turkic nomads rejected subjection to the emerging Ottoman Empire. Instead, they rallied to the messianic Shi'i movement of Shah Ismail Safavi in northwestern Iran. Dissident tribesmen began migrating to the Persian side. The Safavi monarchy emerged out of a messianic religious movement among the Turkoman tribes around 1500. The messianic Safavi leader, Ismail, traveled and recruited in Western Asia, activities which seriously threatened the Ottoman powerbase in Anatolia. The Ottoman Sultan Selim (r.1512–1520) stamped this movement out in his territory with a great massacre of forty thousand Turkmen in 1512 and vigilant persecution thereafter. Meanwhile, the decline of the descendants of Timur (who died in 1405), the disintegration of other Turkish tribal confederacies, and the rise of the Uzbeks in Central Asia created a power vacuum in Western Iran and Azerbaijan. "Safavid Iran was a magnet for those suffering from plague and famine, as well as from Ottoman policies which were antagonistic not only to extremist Shi'a but to nomads and tribes."[13] But the Turkman "tribes" who joined the "Qizilbash" followers of Ismail were already relatively open groups of diverse origins. They were united by their devotion to the charismatic Safavids and to their own nomadic pastoral way of life. They provided quotas of warriors for campaigns—usually in summer—and were allotted particular provinces for their residence and grazing.

But with the stabilization of the Safavids into a kingdom that needed to fend off Ottoman attacks with a permanent army, the role of non-Turkman Iranians and other outsiders increased. Tribesmen had herds and flocks to manage and an unsettling attitude of superiority over townsmen and farmers alike. The turbulent autonomy of the original Qizilbash—the red-capped followers of a messianic leader—could not be tolerated in the new imperial structure. The Safavid dynasty soon found it necessary to quell the tribes that formerly constituted its army and balance them with special palace troops and slave contingents. Thus, Katherine Babayan wrote, it was the "triangular configuration of slave-concubines, eunuchs and military slaves" that forged a network that kept the Safavids in power.[14]

Nonetheless, the dynasty maintained parts of its earlier army under the title "Shahsevan"—devoted to the shah. They had allotted abodes and grazing lands. Over time, their chiefs and nobles usurped the lands allotted to them and distanced themselves from ordinary tribespeople—indeed, oppressed them. This new aristocracy also preferred the amenities of urban life to even the grandest pavilions available to a tribal khan. So, under "the later Safavids, the Qizilbash tribes became increasingly marginalized, and their military contingents were rarely called on." Military exercises and great hunts followed by great feasts were no longer organized. Not surprisingly, "the dynasty, in its last years, had quite lost the ability to rouse the people to devotion." In 1722, the Safavid dynasty was destroyed, and its capital sacked, by a new tribal insurgency, that of the Ghilzai from Afghanistan. The dynasty had made a desperate last appeal, but the response was feeble. Tribal disunity, however, prevented the conquering Ghilzai from establishing a new dominion and they returned with their plunder.

A short period of anarchy followed. The Shahsevan tribes reverted to an autonomous existence on their old grazing lands in northern Iran and Azerbaijan. Many submitted to Russian control during the nineteenth century. But immense areas of Iran were best used by nomadic herdsmen. The weakness of dynasties after the death of Nadir Shah Afshar in 1747 meant that these nomads lived organized in autonomous tribes. Before the early twentieth century, the shah in Tehran had little control over them in their own rangelands.[15] We can illustrate such involuntary relocations and subsequent dispersals with the case of a modern Turkic community, the Shahsevan-e Baghdadi. In 2003, the Shahsevan-e Baghdadi was "a tribal confederacy (él) consisting of two big branches, 'Lek' and 'Arixli', twenty-nine tribes (tayfa), 220 sections (tire) and several hundred sub-sections (göbeg)." All spoke Turkish, and they were Shi'ite Muslims and Iranian nationals. The primary nucleus of this confederacy had been relocated from the suburbs of Kirkuk to Khorassan (or from then northwest to northeast Iran) in 1733 by Nadir, the future shah of Iran. Thereafter, the different tribes and sections of this confederacy dispersed across Iran, Iraq, Turkey, and Syria. The main body migrated to the area of Fars upon the death of Nadir Shah Afshar in 1747. Around 1800, it was settled in Saveh, Qazvin, Hamadan, and nearby areas—that is to say, it was dispersed over several hundred miles. In the later nineteenth century, the Kharaqan Mountains were considered to be the most suitable place for the different tribes of the confederacy, and this area too was handed over to them during the reign of Naser al-Din Shah (r. 1848–1896).[16]

The Iranian monarchy maintained an uneasy relationship with the tribes until massively growing oil revenue, together with external political support and military supplies from the Anglo-American alliance enabled the Pahlavi dynasty (1925–1979), to urbanize and modernize the economy. Autonomous tribes have, for the moment at any rate, dissolved into a larger national organization.

New Tribes from the Ruins of the Chinggisid World Conquest

Since the individual camp or tent cluster was economically and militarily self-contained, tribal fragments could regenerate from each segment. Across Eurasia, stray nomad camps soon coalesced into tenacious new tribes in a few decades after the shattering Mongol conquests had scattered them from the Black Sea to the Sea of Japan. We may take, for example, a modern "tribe" that gave its name to a Soviet-era nationality and modern post-Soviet state. A group named "Uzbek" emerged in the western part of Inner Asia from the wreck of the "tribal state and army," or *ulus*, of Khan Orda. By the end of the fifteenth century, the Uzbek were pressing in upon the cities north of the Amu Darya River. They pushed Babur, the Timurid ruler of Ferghana, out to Kabul and then drove him to ultimately found the Mughal Empire in South Asia (ca. 1526–1857). The Uzbek came under the rule of Abul' Khayr in the 1440s, but two sections migrated east under their own leaders and escaped his control before 1460.

The economic and military organization of these peoples enabled such segmentation. Fragments of these communities then formed smaller raiding bands. Bregel writes that a group "that split off from the Ulus of Abu'l-Khayr became known as Uzbek-Qazaq. The etymology of the word qazaq is unknown, and numerous attempts at establishing it have been unsuccessful."[17] Another authority, Scott Levi, suggests that it meant "free man" or, alternatively, "tribeless."[18] It may have had both connotations—such bands were free from the incipient tyranny of oasis states, even those ruled by their own chiefs. If they fled as individual households, they would indeed be tribeless. But as I have shown, the steppe, while vast, was too densely peopled for isolated camps to survive. The Uzbek-Qazaq grew into a new tribe, and in turn threw up a khan who led the advance into the oases and the cities of desert margins. (Qazaq continued to be used as a term for "free-booter" or "bandit"—but it also ultimately sedimented into a post-Soviet state: today's Kazakhstan.)

Tribal Kingdoms and Khanates in Russian-Dominated Inner Asia

Other branches of the Turkic tribes that founded the Safavid monarchy in Iran and the Ottoman Empire in Eurasia still populated the west-central parts of Inner Asia. They retained the structure of tribal khanates into the last decades of the nineteenth century. Most people lived as seasonal nomads. Khans governed from oasis settlements. They all steadily succumbed to the power of the Russian Empire that had but a few centuries earlier been tributary to the khans of the Golden Horde. Russian expansion began with the conquest of Kazan in 1552, paused owing to the dissolution of the Russian Czarist state into civil war, but was resumed in the 1730s. Disorganized Kazakh tribes could offer little serious resistance to military and economic encroachment.

Russian traders and settlers gradually transformed the region, today's Kazakhstan, which was fully subdued by 1848. Logistical difficulties were the main obstacle to further conquest, but the empire subdued the Turkmen tribes north of the Amu Darya River, and conquered the Uzbek khanates of Khiva, Bukhara, and Kokand. Samarkand, Bukhara, and Merv were taken by 1884. The annexation of Merv prompted the British to intervene diplomatically to mark out the still extant frontier between Russian dominion and the kingdom of Afghanistan. Russian farmers began to colonize the steppes, naturally selecting the most productive land. The now powerless nomadic tribes could not act against the occupation of key grazing land that often included access to water. Cotton farming to supply the Czarist push for industrialization on the British model, was pushed to the extent that the region had to import wheat.[19] The reduction of the Turkic peoples from tribal khanates continued and was intensified under the Soviet Union. The immensely powerful Soviet regime could force well-adapted pastoral nomads to settle as cotton farmers and starve. But thousands of families took their herds and fled across the still open frontiers of Afghanistan and Iran.[20] The USSR reorganized Central Asia into five republics, each allotted a specific ethnicity and language. Its power dissolved traditional organization but sometimes, as Findlay remarks, ended up recreating "the old micropolitics of clan and retinue."[21]

The Russian empire also steadily expanded eastward to the limits newly established by the Qing rulers a century earlier. The Amur River frontier was established in 1689. The Russians built the Trans-Siberian railroad and tightened their military grip upon the oasis states of Central Asia. Thus, by 1900, the growing Russian Empire had pushed against the limits of the Turkic dominions of the Qing Empire in the east.

A Mongol Fragment—the Hazara of Afghanistan

I have emphasized how the whirlwind unleashed by Chinggis Khan reforged the peoples of Inner Asia into radically new organizations. The decay of Mongol dominion left sections of these peoples scattered across Asia. One of these groups is named Hazara—literally "thousand"— evidence that it originated as a contingent in the Mongol armies. They may have been stranded in central Afghanistan by the decay of the Mongol Empire. Their several tribes retained strong traditions of Mongol descent in the 1950s, when a Danish team studied their regional culture. Their language in the twentieth century was a variety of Persian with a high admixture of Mongol words not found in other languages spoken in Afghanistan. Scattered groups merely described themselves as "Moghol." These groups declared, not implausibly, that they had arrived in two phases, one with Chinggis (which would be ca. 1220) and the second with "Tīmūr Kuragān" (known in the West as "Tamerlane"), who died in 1405.

Atwood believes the Hazara to be the result of a merger of the Qara'una Mongol ruling elite with regional peasant communities. Their military contingents formed an important part of Timur's armies around 1400. But they were gradually isolated by the rise of the Mughal and Safavid Empires. Shah Abbas of Persia (1587–1629) then persuaded them to accept an elder of his choosing. It is perhaps from this period that those in the Hazara heartland turned strongly toward Shi'i ideas. Their isolation was accentuated by their decision to adopt the Iranian Shi'i version of Islam. They also lived in difficult mountain country that was only subdued by the king of Afghanistan in the 1880s and 1890s.[22] But even among them, the Persian-speaking seminomads (*Chahar Aimaq*) were mainly Sunni.

Leadership, however, remained in the hands of their tribal chiefs, or *mirs*. Some Hazara tribes collaborated with the British during their invasion between 1878 and 1880. The then king of Afghanistan, Abdurrahman, decided to take strong measures to assert his authority. The chiefs were required to submit and the Amir was to station troops in their country. Central authority was harshly imposed. The Hazaras were required to surrender their weapons. Then the king ordered that the chiefs and religious class should be separated and sent to live under surveillance in Kabul. The objective clearly was to break Hazara social structure by removing their leadership. This action provoked an uprising that was mercilessly crushed. Their distinct version of Islam, as well as their political resistance, led the Amir Abd al-Rahman to permit his armies, and the numerous Pashtun volunteers who joined them, to not only seize the Hazaras' goods, but also to enslave many of the survivors.[23] In the 1950s, Ferdinand recorded that the chiefs were largely submissive to the royal government.

In the 1950s, they were divided into three clusters: Hazara, "*Chahar Aimaq*" (meaning "four tribes/armies"), and one described only as "Moghol." When the community was studied in the 1950s, the first group were located in Badakshan and identified as an Uzbek subtribe. The second included all the Moghols of western Afghanistan. The latter came to be known as "*Moghol Shahjahan*" because they were supposed to have joined Shahjahan in his attacks on India. (Shah Jahan was in reality the sixth Mughal emperor. He ruled from Delhi and in fact sent an expedition *from* India to capture Qandahar.)

Klaus Ferdinand described the Shahjahan group as "pashtunnized" (i.e., having adopted Pashtun or Pakhtun culture). They were nomads who lived in black tents like the nomadic Pashtun. There was general agreement on three of the "Four aimaq" groupings, but the fourth was variously named in different areas. The idea of its diverse origins was accepted. This was reflected in the *aimaq* name *Jamshedi*. One etymologically false but deeply meaningful folk etymology was that it derived from *jama shud*—"it is collected." The aggregation was attributed to Chinggis. He and his immediate successors certainly dragooned diverse people into new military followings, though this specific one may have formed later. It is, however, noteworthy that, despite their admittedly diverse origins, all Hazaras, like most Afghans in the 1950s, were affiliated to a recognized tribe (*Dāy*) with its own leadership structure. Ferdinand quotes a proverb that "A Hazāra without a *Dāy* is like an Afghan without a *–zai*." (The *zai* termination indicated the name of the larger tribal to which a man's family belonged.) This meant that it was as rare to meet a Hazara who did not belong to a certain tribe as to meet a detribalized Afghan.[24] The Hazara now exist as a stigmatized minority in Afghanistan.

Making the Manchus into a Ruling "Tribe"

The history of the Mongols served as inspiration and warning for a new borderland polity that emerged from Liaodong and the western borderlands of Korea in the 1500s. This region had—like much of the world—been overrun and subjugated by the Mongols, who destroyed the Jin imperial dynasty that had ruled in North China before the Mongols' arrival. Remaining Jurchen were organized into a subunit, a province of the Mongol Empire. This area remained loosely subordinated to the Ming Empire that replaced the Yuan after 1368.

Communities in Manchuria were not steppe nomads. This was an area with an ecological-political mosaic where small egalitarian tribes of pastoralists coexisted with hunters and sedentary communities. They supported themselves by tillage, animal husbandry, and hunting. The mix varied with habitat. Powerful leaders periodically forged tribal formations that then established large states in North China, or even conquered the whole of it. Some chieftains connected themselves ancestrally with the Jin emperors but simply aspired to a privileged position in the Ming trade and tribute system. Pamela Crossley describes how new polities in tension with the Ming Empire developed in the northeast in Liaodong (also known as Nurgan) by 1600 CE. The khanate from which the Qing Empire took shape lay "at the eastern edge of Liaodong, at the heart of a world dominated by Ming soldiers and Jurchen traders." There were many Jurchen there, but also Han Chinese, Koreans, and other groups. Lineage organization and loyalty were sociopolitically vital for defense and offense. But this was exactly the reason they were unstable. As Crossley points out, they "were constantly formed and reformed through the social and economic processes of life in the Jurchen territories." Having remote kinsfolk was no help to families in a specific settlement. Therefore, settlers would use the name of a village or locality as a "lineage name." In some cases, this echoed the name of lineage founders who gave the site their family name. So residents in the Ma family village would have "Magiya" as the family name thereafter. Nomenclature and affiliation thus changed as circumstances required.[25]

One of the Jurchen was the ambitious chieftain Nurgaci, who was initially simply lord of a large village. He steadily expanded his power over his neighbors of various ethnicities. Around 1595, Nurgaci began shaping a key institution of the future Manchu dynasty—the "banner" as a social and military unit composed of warriors and their families. He and other rulers also began abducting peasants from Ming imperial territory and settling them as serf farmers under their own rule. Yet other peasants voluntarily fled into their lands. The strengthened Khan Nurgaci and his successor, Hung Taiji, carried off thousands of people from Ming territory. One Ming frontier official described how this enhanced the striking power of the emerging rival empire. Formerly, he wrote, there was little fodder in the winter and spring, so nomads' horses were as thin as sticks and they could not mount raids into Ming territory in that season. But by 1620, a great chief might have several thousand captive or refugee serfs; a lesser one had at least a thousand. They tilled the land and paid tribute in grain and fodder. The rulers' horses and men were always well-fed and could march at any time. He also reported that border people considered their taxes would be lighter than those of the Ming government and discussed fleeing into Jurchen territory. Shortly thereafter, Nurgaci, the emerging Jurchen khan, inflicted a severe defeat on the Ming and drove them south of the Great Wall. Effectively, he had created a state that controlled Liaodong and looked back on the Jin Jurchen Empire of four centuries earlier as a model.

Many of the young men captured from the Ming lands were drafted willy-nilly into military 'Banners'; other households were redistributed among the lords and commanders of the emerging state and used as needed. Literate men might rise to command positions. Nurgaci's distrust of the indecipherable calligraphy of those literati, however, also led him to command the creation of a separate Manchu script in 1599. This was to be used to write their native language, just as Mongolian was written in a Mongol script created for that purpose during their empire.[26]

Nurgaci's son, Hung Taiji, came to power in 1626 and developed an even wider imperial strategy. His kingdom grew into a great power that overthrew the Ming and, over several decades, conquered the whole of China. Nurgaci had sorted lineages and individuals into his empire on a functional basis. Paradoxically, Hung Taiji began to construct genealogical segments and to assign tasks to individuals depending on their supposed descent. People were classed as those from beyond the Great Wall and those south of it. In the military units that conquered China, Mongols were separated from the new Manchu ethnicity and so were "martial Chinese" units, even though all of them had played a major role in the conquest. This shaping of a dominant ethnicity from out of the mixed armies of a dramatically successful conquest regime was accompanied by a recasting of terminology. Ranks and offices within the banners were given new "Manchu" names to replace those of too obviously Chinese derivation.

The Qing independently developed Ibn Khaldun's understanding of the natural military value of agrarian-pastoral peoples. But unlike him, they also had a policy solution to prevent the cycle of urban luxury and dynastic decay that he outlined. Their initial conquest of China was built upon the Mongol legacy of reshaping soldiers into permanent service units. The Mongol khans had drastically sorted their subject peoples into new service groupings that then became the frame for "tribal" organizations after the fall of the Mongol Empire. The Mongols had placed their garrisons across North China, taking over large tracts of land for grazing. The Qing were aware of these precedents but carried out a more drastic process of social engineering. They sought to govern their vast empire *as though* a set of tribally organized armies had conquered it. The banners were not in fact, originally tribal units at all. But during the conquest phase, they were briefly shaped into far-ranging militarized tribes. No other premodern regime had the boldness or the administrative capacity to attempt such a project. In this way, loose, existing followings composed of captives, dependents, retainers, and kin were now ordered and sorted according to political need into descent groups. The banner armies were initially deployed wherever they were needed, from Mongolia to Szechwan and beyond.

Once the empire stabilized in the Kangxi reign, the emperors also began a steady process of identifying and separating the Chinese-martial units that had formed a large part of the original conquest armies from the Manchu and Mongols. This amounted to the creation of "Manchus" out of the array of bands and tribes that conquered an empire. The process depended vitally on writing and records, even retrospectively rewritten ones. The Qing sought to develop a trustworthy literate conquest elite by encouraging literacy in both Chinese and Manchu among the bannermen and encouraging them with quotas in the civil service examinations. It also set up a total of 106 permanent garrisons of Manchu bannermen. But unlike the Mongols in their heyday, they generally did not leave the support and provisioning of these men to either the chances of plunder or the labor of noncombatant tribespeople following with the flocks and herds. Specific provision was made for banner garrisons with large tracts of confiscated lands allotted for their support. These ultimately proved insufficient for them and began to be supplemented with cash grants.[27]

Peter Perdue has described how the eighteenth-century Qing were expanding into Inner Asia. The Qing had already subdued the peoples around the extended mixed-farming and pastoral rimlands of agrarian China, from Manchuria to Xinjiang. In the arid lands of Inner Asia, garrisons were also supported by military farm colonies. These were subsidized by tax revenues from Eastern China. "The vast distances, barren deserts, and low-yielding lands of the frontier had hitherto protected the nomads" against most reprisals. But now the Qing rulers were reaching deep into the deserts and steppes with their new wealth and armies.[28] The interpenetration of tribal and "banner" structures still occasionally occurred. In 1733 and 1734, the chieftain of the Turfan area beat off the regional Zunghar ruler. But he feared a new attack and prudently evacuated his small oasis. Nearly 10,000 people migrated to Chinese protection and were formed into a "banner" unit, with Amin Khwaja, the chief, as their commander.[29] The Qing suffered a setback with the reestablishment of a rebel khanate based in Yarkand, but this was then crushed by a renewed military campaign, now equipped with European firearms, in the 1870s.

While they vacillated about it, the Qing emperors generally sought to reserve the Liaodong area north of the Great Wall as a preserve where the Manchu should lead a rustic life and preserve their military virtues. They would also populate the region and check Russian expansion. But efforts to return them to Manchuria to sustain themselves in traditional ways and regain their martial qualities ultimately failed. The great majority of those sent there deserted back to China proper.[30]

Thus, the creation of the Manchu banner people as a socially bounded community may be considered an immense project in social engineering. While it was not described as such, we can understand the Kangxi emperor's effort to strictly separate the "martial Chinese" banners from the "Manchu" as an effort to prioritize lineage descent as the criterion of identity and to require cultural traits, such as names and languages, to fit into it. Furthermore, in this project, the purified Manchu were to acquire the literacy skills to rule a complex society, but also retain their original military virtues. It was a strategy to first create tribal units and then install them as a powerful elite across a great agrarian empire *as though* it had been conquered by an ethnically distinct tribe, who then formed a ruling caste.

The effort ultimately failed. Despite their landed estates, banner garrisons first lapsed into a privileged caste and then decayed into a marginal minority. The effort to raise an elite among them to be seamlessly both martial Manchu bowmen and refined Chinese literati largely failed.[31] By the mid-nineteenth century, banner armies proved unable to cope with Chinese rebels, not to speak of Western invaders. Meanwhile, as we saw in chapter 2, the identification of "Manchu" as a conquering descent group briefly made them targets for "Chinese" nationalism in the last decades of the Qing Empire.

This Qing Empire took considerable pains to enlist Mongols in its armies and to neutralize those who were not enlisted. The Qing also initially applied the ideal of followership to determine "Mongol" identity. But as the empire moved from a conquest state to a tightly structured administration, Crossley observed that they adopted linguistic unity and standardization as *the* defining criterion. By doing this, they were (in the eighteenth century!) already moving to a "modern" or even contemporary definition of a Mongol ethnic group. Some kinds of membership were more valuable than others. Only those enrolled in the Mongol military "banners" received stipends from the shrinking coffers of the state while others were left to fend for themselves.[32] At the same time, imperial policy sought to multiply the number of small Mongol administrative units in the Mongolian lands at the periphery so as to preclude their posing a unified challenge to the empire. Thus, by the mid-eighteenth century, Mongolia, Turkestan, and Chinghai had no less than 149 administrative banners under nineteen khans. The possibility of Mongols again coalescing under one leader was firmly foreclosed.[33] The imperial court progressively turned toward a rigid taxonomy of descent lines (*zu*) to distinguish between Han, Manchu, Mongol, or Tibetan, each with a specific language and set of names. Linguistic ethnicization in lands that had historically threatened the Chinese imperial center was thus an aspect of political detribalization.

The Southwest in Ming-Qing Times

We may recollect that lands of Southwest China or Northwest Zomia were moist enough to be adaptable to Chinese-style farming, especially after the introduction of New World crops in the 1500s. These were inhabited (to invoke Fiskesjö again) by assimilable Raw peoples. The imperial Ming dynasty began to consolidate itself in the southwestern borderlands earlier subjugated by the Mongols, but refrained for several decades from registering households for administrative purposes. It instead encouraged local tribal chiefs to raise militia units for imperial service. It was not, therefore, an immediately pressing issue to distinguish between Yao tribespeople and *min*; that is to say, "between nontax-paying, hill-dwelling people and the emperor's subjects. That was a distinction created by government registration, and only thereafter did Ming officials have to distinguish between the indigenous natives who came under native officials and those who did not."

But state action also promoted acculturation to a perceived Han norm. Registration in official records was followed among the upwardly mobile by the construction of ancestral halls where approved sacrifices were conducted. This was accompanied by a claim to descent from immigrants from the imperial heartland in the north. These processes began to create an ethnic boundary between Yao and Chinese. Similar processes shaped the boundary between Zhuang, governed by their local officials (chieftains), and Han, governed by transferrable officials appointed by the emperor.[34] Submission, but also cultural adaptation and insertion into the standard imperial system, separated "tribal" and "non-tribal" peoples. But it was an ideology of lineal descent manifested in permanent buildings and regular rituals that provided the "mental map" through which these boundaries were marked. In some cases, lineages formally identified with temples were originally established by Ming military garrisons.[35]

Frank Dikötter agrees with Crossley that group identity through patrilineal descent became important in the Qianlong period (1736–1795). But even in the closely administered lands of South China, Michael Szonyi has observed that large descent lineages traced through many generations were especially numerous. This he attributes to the geographic and ethnic "frontier" character of Han Chinese expansion into these areas in previous centuries.[36] Within three distinct social levels—popular culture, gentry society, and court politics—the common notion of patrilineal descent came to be deployed on a widespread scale in the creation and maintenance of group boundaries.[37] Meanwhile, in the provinces within the Great Wall, there was, as Dikötter writes:

> a consolidation of the cult of patrilineal descent, centre of a broad movement of social reform that emphasized family and lineage (*zu*). Considerable friction arose between lineages throughout the nineteenth century in response to heightened competition over natural resources, the need to control market towns, the gradual erosion of social order and organization problems caused by demographic pressures. The militarization of powerful lineages reinforced folk models of kinship solidarity, forcing in turn more loosely organized associations to form a unified descent group under the leadership of the gentry. At court level too, ideologies of descent became increasingly significant, in particular with the erosion of a sense of cultural identity among Manchu aristocrats—the founders of the Qing dynasty in 1644.[38]

With administrative breakdown and the rise of major rebellions like the Taiping and Nien, it would seem that some prominent Chinese lineages began to manage local security. As in all military situations, lineage heads had to double as local "strong men." It is heretical to suggest it, but were Chinese lineages moving to becoming "proto-tribes" themselves? If so, however, the development was cut short in the twentieth century.

Tribes and Ethnic Minorities in the People's Republic

The Qing Empire's remarkable efforts at ethnic reshaping were feeble when compared with the massive social engineering carried out under the People's Republic of China after 1949. It systematized "nationalities" in an unprecedented way. The Republic was determined to be composed of exactly fifty-six nationalities, of which the Han comprised over 90 percent of the population. Mullaney has described how the hundreds of "nationality" (*minzu*) names reported were reduced to fifty-five plus one. He also uncovered how communities with different names and no strong sense of having a transcommunity identity were molded into a single group by pressure and persuasion.[39]

The PRC's project drew upon the intellectual legacies of Republican China, as well as the unacknowledged work of a British ethnographer. It, however, abandoned the GMD (KMT) regime's insistence that all the people of the republic were one nationality. But the official line deployed the terminological structure of a Soviet-type Marxism-Leninism absorbed after World War I. Not surprisingly, J. V. Stalin was a major doctrinal source for the latter. While a minor Bolshevik leader, J. V. Stalin wrote an essay in 1913 on what constituted a "nation." A nation did not, he wrote, have a racial or tribal basis. His definition was: "A nation is a historically constituted, stable community of people, formed on the basis of a common language, territory, economic life, and psychological make-up manifested in a common culture."[40] By 1950, when pronouncing on language, he saw it as emerging in an early state of social evolution, one marked by the existence of tribe as a precursor of nationality. "History tells us," he wrote, "that the languages of these tribes and nationalities were not class languages, but languages common to the whole of a tribe or nationality, and understood by all its people."[41]

The PRC thus inherited from its Western forebears, Marxist and non-Marxist, a primordialist notion of "society," "people," or "nationality" and language. At least for Stalin, these terms had a linguistic but also cultural basis. Social structure was thus seen as corresponding to a "stage" of social development. For his followers in the PRC, *shizu* and *buluo* corresponded to "clan" and "tribe"—both were characteristic of "primordial communism." The *minzu* existed under both capitalism and socialism. These, of course, were used to describe the twentieth-century condition of China.[42]

This background was manifest in debates about particular peoples, especially in South China. These areas were known to have been settled by several waves of Han in recent history. An earlier—and culturally distinct wave—formed the "Hakka" ethnic group. We may see this, for example, in the case of the She peoples.

"Debates persisted on whether the She were actually Han people until the early 1950s, when the She were designated an official 'national minority.'" Various features of Hakka society—such as the participation of women in heavy physical labor—were then explained as resulting from Han people having to adapt to the customs of the "aboriginal She." Indeed, even an unusual pattern of Hakka family names was explained as having been assigned to powerless immigrants by powerful She magnates or chiefs.[43] Thus, many of the features of the concept of aboriginal tribes became embedded in the concept of a national minority, especially along China's southwest frontier zone in the rugged mountains and narrow valleys of the Southeast Asian Massif. But the PRC saw it as a largely bygone stage in the social evolution of the minority people, one which the Han had already surpassed. The exceptionally powerful and organized PRC, however, appears to have largely erased any separate "tribal" formations in its territory. This provides a marked contrast to the South Asian situation over roughly the same period.

French Colonial Indochina

South and southeast of the modern Szechwan border lay various ethnically and geographically lands colonized by the French and British in the nineteenth century. Only Siam (Thailand) survived as a sovereign entity. The French in Indochina abutted directly on Qing imperial territory. Their northward expansion through Vietnam and Laos however suffered a stinging defeat at Lam Song in 1885 at the hands of a coalition of hill peoples aided by Chinese soldiers from Szechwan. The French ministry led by Jules Ferry that had advocated a "forward policy" fell from power. The affronted metropolitan government could not afford another humiliation just after its defeat by Germany in 1871. So the new government poured resources into subduing the people and demarcating the frontier. By 1896, French colonial authorities had captured most of the "bandit" chiefs and secured Chinese agreement on demarcating the frontier. But subduing the area took far longer.

Military officers were instructed to carry out ethnographic surveys and generate maps so that the colonial authorities could properly regulate the various communities labeled *Montagnards*, meaning "hill people." Linguistic and ethnic mapping was adjusted to suit the colonial strategy of allying with certain "friendly" groups while promoting division amongst "less well-controlled groups." At the same time, just as in British territory, an inner-line frontier was drawn to separate plains peasants from the mountain zones that were kept under military control.[44]

All states have dealt with the Zomia region by different mixtures of coercion and conciliation. The region was largely subdued by the English and French empires only around World War I. Its fall to the Japanese between 1941 and 1943 marked the beginning of the colonial retreat from Asia. This upland region of sharply dissected mountains and narrow valleys has long interacted with major empires and successor states: the Chinese, Vietnamese, Lao, Thai, Burman, Indian, and Bangladeshi. The Tai-speaking peoples, known as Shan, spread from today's southwest China and established many small kingdoms across the "mid-altitude lands" of the massif. These were based on permanent wet-rice cultivation. They enlarged their range after the Yuan (Mongol) dynasty shattered the older kingdoms of central Burma without establishing a stable domain of its own. Their expansion was checked by a resurgent kingdom of Burma in the sixteenth century.

British Rule in Burma

British colonial rule began in Bengal (which then included today's Bangladesh) in the 1750s. It inherited the late Mughal administration of deltaic Bengal, but only gradually became aware that the region was permeated with networks of monastic establishments. Several of the most important and powerful of these extended into the Himalaya and connected with Buddhist sites and establishments there. The latter exercised a loose tributary power through peripatetic disciples and traders. These networks of armed trade were frequently linguistically Tibeto-Burman as well as Bengali. Their working also ran counter to the concept of complete territorial sovereignty that the new colonial government sought to impose. They were, therefore, identified early in British records as either insurgents and bandits within British territory or "savage tribes" on its borders. Clashes began in the 1770s, but the erosion of these networks was a protracted task. But the establishment of British-run tea plantations in many of the best swidden lands made the task more important for colonial authority, and a steady pressure was maintained for over a century.[45] This radically transformed the ethnic and religious landscape and led to the emergence of "modern" tribal structures by the end of colonial rule in 1947. But the new Republic of India has been faced with various forms of resistance in the area ever since. These have been managed by both direct repression involving large forces from the regular army. Alongside it however have gone more or less successful efforts at accommodation through power-sharing and financial subsidies.[46] The long-running insurgency in the state of Nagaland was only pacified by permitting one guerilla movement to collect 'taxes' from business and professions, including employees of the government of India who were stationed in the state. This was formalized in 1997 and has continued to the present.[47]

British colonial rule in the lower, or the southern deltaic part of Burma (now Myanmar) began in 1824 after clashes between the two states on the eastern border of British Bengal. Additional portions of Burma were occupied in 1854 and exploited for the still rich teak forests to be found there. Finally, the British annexed the northern part of the kingdom of Burma to their empire in 1885. They faced years of rural insurgency, especially in the hill forests. They gradually created a belt of relatively subservient "Shan states" along the northeast borderland of Burma.

This was the setting studied by Edmund Leach, whose comparative fieldwork was aided by his years of military service in the area during World War II. Leach showed how the Kachin, described by early officials as ethnically distinct hill people, had often dominated Shan Valley communities. He also showed that individuals and families crossed this ethnic divide from time to time. The new colonial administration after 1885 made great efforts to segregate the communities as part of its efforts at enforcing its own laws. On the other hand, the hill communities' religious life was not organized under the leadership of the Buddhist clergy as that of the lowland Burmese was. They were therefore more open to missionary enterprise: for example, a number of Karen tribespeople converted to Christianity and were educated in mission schools. A few Karen rose to high positions in the British civil service and military. Others formed part of the rank and file of the colonial army, replicating the pattern already established in India with the Gurkha community of Nepal who provided a large fraction of the British Indian army. "Karen joined the British army in substantial numbers, helping to suppress Burmese rebellions in 1886 and 1930–1932." Burma became independent of the British in 1947, but soon lapsed into a dictatorship. The centralizing military government that ruled Burma/Myanmar from the 1960s to recent times attempted to assert its control over the northeast of the country, sparking an insurgency among the Karen that still continues today. [48]

The war in French Indochina broke out in 1945, and much of the fighting occurred in mountain regions. Even in countries not directly affected by the war, such as Thailand, this led to intensive efforts to "uplift" and integrate tribal communities in order to prevent the spread of communist ideas among them. At the turn of the century, leaders among these communities began to reject the idea of being "Hill Tribes" and claimed the title of "Indigenous People." This claim then had to be documented to the satisfaction of the Thai government. [49]

Caste Systems and Tribal Conquests

The structures of conquest tribes in the agrarian heartland of the Indian subcontinent offer an interesting comparison to the Manchu example. They additionally present the working out of social organization along a tribe-caste continuum. I will illustrate that social logic through a detailed presentation of Barth's study of a conquest community that became a dominant caste *even in an entirely Muslim society*. It illustrates, in my view, the structural underpinnings, as distinct from the elaborated ideologies, of caste systems.

Around 1500, a new tribe, the Yusufzai, a branch of the Pashtun or Pathan peoples, conquered the Swat Valley in today's Northwest Pakistan. Thus, they constituted a relatively new conquest elite at the beginning of the sixteenth century. These Pathans traced their ancestry to the mythic ancestor of all Afghans, Qais, through Yusuf, the eponymous ancestor of the Yusufzai. Exact genealogical memory in the Swat Valley, however, was socially institutionalized only with the sixteenth-century conquest of the valley. After that, all claims to landownership and consequent political dominance stemmed from that conquest. According to their legend, a holy man, Sheikh Malli, ended internecine disputes after victory by allotting the valley among all the recognized descendants of Yusuf, the tribal ancestor. These were divided into thirteen branches sorted "in terms of their relations to each other through their closer patrilineal ancestors." The rights of each branch were then shared by their major segments. All landowners (in the 1950s) could still be located within this genealogical structure: each one belonged to a named khel, or major tribal segment. "Every unit of land is thought of as a 'share,' a portion of a larger estate held by a descent group of Pakhtuns. This estate is referred to as daftar; an individual's daftar is his inherited share of it as a member of the descent group. There is thus a direct connexion between the descent organization and rights to land."

Everyone who did not hold such a share was a dependent, and not a regular member of the Yusufzai tribe. Thus, Barth observed, the property system emphasized the distance between the conquerors and their subjects. Social distance was intensified, as he wrote:

> by the restrictions on intermarriage which lead to the development of social groups of a caste type. . . . Landowners, as a group, thus tend to marry endogamously, but they also take some women in marriage from lower groups, whereas they will not give their daughters in marriage to inferiors. . . . This hierarchical type of category is usually called qoum—people, religious or ethnic group, caste. The different qoums of Swat constitute patrilineal, hereditary, ranked occupational groups, conceptually endogamous. Each qoum is named, and membership in a qoum is unalterably determined by birth. Sociologically they might be classified as estates or castes.

Different occupational groups were tied together by permanent obligations to assist in the cultivation of specific landowners' fields. Cultivation, at minimum, required (apart from the actual plowman) the resources and labor of several specialists, including the carpenter who made and mended the plow, the rope-maker who provided cordage, and the smith who made and repaired tools. All this was coordinated by the landowner who took the main share of the crop, with the artisans receiving their shares from him. The system, Barth noted, strengthened the authority of the chief and the solidarity of the unit he controlled.[50]

Genealogies provided the framework for the political and social life of the tribes and of the kingdom of Afghanistan whose political life they collectively constituted. That in turn ensured the reproduction of genealogy as the approved form of social memory in the region and beyond. Afghan soldiers migrating across South Asia carried the pattern of genealogical memory with them into lands where they came as a conquest elite. They felt themselves effectively a dominant minority among a larger population. It is not surprising that Elphinstone also generally singled out the Yusufzai tribe among the Afghans for their overbearing ways. It served to mark them out as a 'dominant caste' in the Indian system of caste ranking.[51]

The Shaping of a Rohilla Tribe and Territory in North India

Displays of dominance could be parlayed into military employment and actual power. By the late eighteenth century, the Rohillas were a well-recognized Afghan tribe—but they were found only in India! Paradoxically, there was no such name in Afghanistan, nor even a region or village from which that name might be derived. Elphinstone, who made his inquiries around 1810, could only guess that the name derived from the Panjabi word meaning "a hill." He added that it was only known to "some of the Afghauns through the medium of books written in India."[52] An Irish officer in the Maratha service in southern India described the bearers of this name in 1796. The Rohillas, he wrote, "are all Mussulmans…men of tried courage, and generally reserved for storming or some such desperate service; they do no other duty whatever, and have not even the shadow of discipline among them."

The Rohillas thus provide a more recent and better documented example of the creation of a tribe that then became a lordly elite, the *Arthashastra*'s military *sangha* under another name. This occurred not in the secluded borderlands of Afghanistan, but in long-settled lands of the upper Gangetic Plain. Jos Gommans has scrutinized the early history of the community in North India. He observes that being a Rohilla was not a question of birth, but attainable through a mixture of performance, alliance and patronage. Gommans presents this as part of a long-extant pattern of eastward migration of men accustomed to the use of horses and arms, moving from the Afghan borderlands to the plains. He claims with some hyperbole that "Yusufzai state-formation actually came into its own in Katehr [the Rohilla regional center] in northern India."[53]

There was however nothing particularly Yusufzai about the new dominant community in what became Rohilkhand. Daud was adopted by a merchant who lived in Kandahar. Daud migrated to the plains of North India. Presumably possessing that "affectation of military pride and ferocity" that Elphinstone noted as characteristic of Afghan bearing in India, he enlisted as a mercenary soldier in the service of a local raja. He soon proved himself in battle and military successes enlarged his following. Many Afghan soldiers of fortune joined him. He captured a young boy while raiding a village and later adopted him under the name of Ali Muhammad Khan. After Daud's death, the latter secured the support of his Afghan followers and gradually enlarged his possessions. His followers gradually acquired superior landlord rights across the entire region. They generally obliterated all superior tenures as far as possible and thus installed themselves as ruling landlord elite.[54] Elphinstone visited one of their settlements and remarked on the numbers of robust young men he saw reclining in lordly ease in the town.

An analogous dominant elite based on conquest and descent—in this case allegedly from a single conqueror around 1600—was the Rajput landlord elite of a cluster of seventy villages near the city of Banaras. In the 1950s, Bernard Cohn was told that all the lands in the village and the land throughout the taluka or sub-district followed the descent line from the conqueror Ganesh Rai. "Every adult male Thakur can trace his descent from this ancestor. Two Dobhi Thakurs meeting for the first time will sit down and compare their formal relationship and appropriate behavior to each other."[55]

Late Empire and Early Republic in India

Expanding markets, dramatically improved communications, and the enlarged representative capacity of the colonial state led to a growing body of colonial law intended to insulate "tribes" from the forces of colonial modernity. Furthermore, the British Empire in India was also waging an ideological war with its nationalist critics beginning in the late nineteenth century. One of the strategies employed was to delegitimize its Indian critics by labeling them upper-class malcontents with no interest in the welfare of the masses. Gandhi's resort to mass peasant agitation from 1916 onward intensified efforts to control nationalists' access to forest-dwelling communities. That did not protect them from government employees, though. The activist anthropologist Verrier Elwin wrote, "I cannot think of anything more shameful, anything meaner, anything more disgraceful to an administration that claims to be enlightened than the way subordinates openly rob these poor people, some of the poorest in the world, of the few goods they have and of many hours of [forced] labour."[56] Protection against "other Indians" did not protect against the minions of the state, then or after the formation of the Indian Republic in 1950.

Colonial ethnology had also led to a classification of peoples as having distinct traits and capacities. Sometimes the unconscious legacy of racial theory also affected classification. In 1960, the Census of India commissioned a number of village and community studies. One of these was of the Siddis, a Muslim community of Gujarat who were mainly descended from slaves of East African origin. The study began by saying that they were the only ethnic group in mainland India "which possess uncontroverted and well-defined Negroid features." In fact, this seems to have been the only basis for their classification as a tribe. Otherwise, they were simply poor Gujarati farmers, fishermen, and migrant laborers, like many others in the region.[57]

As Nandini Sundar elegantly summarized it, a still unresolved debate continues between "anthropology's salvage instincts, the symbiosis between functionalism and [imperial] indirect rule, and the legal framework instituted . . . in response to Adivasi rebellions."

The 1935 Government of India Act, which granted a limited representative government in much of British India, therefore "reserved" certain constituencies for the "aboriginals." This practice was continued in the constitution of the Indian Republic promulgated in 1950, which, however, introduced universal adult suffrage. But while rival agendas of insulation or integration were debated, Sundar points out, market forces and political currents were sweeping across the perceived boundaries. As the reach of the federal and state governments expanded during the twentieth century, state employment became more accessible and more desirable. Rural life on dwindling landholdings and with eroding common resources became much harder. The great majority of India's Scheduled Tribes are, as Sundar has pointed out, settled agriculturists. Those who are not are often casual laborers in agriculture or construction.[58]

Banjaras versus Gonds: Militarized Merchants Become a Dominant Aboriginal Tribe

When the future emperor Babur began his rise along the western Indus Valley, most of the land was being used by itinerant cattle-keepers. He wrote in vexation that this livestock formed the only plunder available and that his men ruined their horses galloping after them. Cattle were so abundant that a mere servant could seize three or four hundred during the march.[59] It is perhaps not coincidental that a major community of nomadic herdsmen were known as Multanis—people from southern Panjab. This area also adjoined the arid desert of Marwar. It was the language of this region that was spoken by the community of caravan people who ranged across the Indian subcontinent in the eighteenth century. The British needed them to supply their armies, and the earliest published study by John Briggs considered them in this light. Briggs wrote that a "proprietor," or family head, usually owned from four or five to 200 cattle. In the 1860s and 1870s, James Forsyth wrote, these herdsmen were to be found trading salt and other goods across the forested regions of Central India. He added that though "eminent in the art and practice of highway robbery, the Banjaras are scrupulously faithful in the execution of trusts, and are constantly employed in the interchange of commodities between the open country and the forest tracts." He thought they bore no resemblance to either the "Hindus" or to any of the known aboriginal tribes.[60]

Every maximal Banjara tribe was composed of individual camps, each under its own chief. Like pastoral nomads elsewhere, tribes often claimed to control specific territorial ranges. This control was sometimes contested, and John Briggs, who interviewed many nomads between 1806 and 1810, was told of bloody conflicts between them. Cases of such battles are found in the Marathi records as well. The autonomy of these military nomads was recognized by the Maratha rulers at the time (1740–1741). Their violence was only punished because a government clerk was accidentally killed in the affray.[61]

Regardless of the size of the band, each chief of a household cluster claimed a share in the decisions of the encamped tribe or *tanda*. In times of great demand for their services, gatherings containing 30,000 oxen might be assembled through section chiefs. This was indeed an "acephalous" or tribal political structure— one with power diffused among many leaders, great and small. Finally, Banjara bands not only grazed their cattle where they chose, but also domineered over village communities. They hyperbolically claimed that Asaf Jah, the first Nizam of Hyderabad, had given them the right to seize roof thatch for fodder, water from pitchers to drink, and even advance pardon for five murders daily.

The whole political structure strongly resembles that of the classic Inner Asian nomads, as does their partly predatory relation to agricultural communities they moved among. But in contrast to steppe pastoralists, the Banjaras were not even notionally self-sufficient. They had adapted to a niche in the political economy of South Asia and used seasonal grazing to fuel their transport service. They moved salt, grain, or military supplies as required. They claimed Rajput or warrior caste descent, were always armed, and could also supplement their commerce with robbery.[62] But after Indian independence, their social and cultural distinctness was leveraged to secure a declaration that they were an indigenous tribe in the South Indian state of Andhra Pradesh.

This status was then used to occupy lands belonging to an older tribal community, the Gonds. The name Gond refers to various sections of a large group of tribes living in the eastern part of the central Indian forests, now under the administration of several states. They were ethnically distinct from the peasant population of the plains. Several kingdoms emerged here in the fifteenth and sixteenth centuries before succumbing to the Mughal Empire. Kingdoms reemerged in the eighteenth century, but internal strife led to the development of tributary relations with the Maratha kingdom of Nagpur. The latter was annexed to the British Empire in 1854. Part of the Gond territory was allocated to the protected feudatory state of Hyderabad. In 1948 the state was merged into the Indian Republic.[63]

An anthropologist with long experience in the area, Fürer-Haimendorf, described the beginning of Banjara expansion in the 1940s. The Banjaras "employed their greater business sense and their powerful physique to bully and intimidate their Gond neighbours." They thus acquired considerable areas of land formerly occupied by Gonds. This suffered a check when government rules prohibiting transfers of "tribally owned land" to non-tribal people were promulgated in 1975. But then, in 1976, the Banjaras were able to get themselves added to the list of Scheduled Tribes in the state of Andhra Pradesh. The regulations could not be used against them, and they were also able to secure large state allotments of land intended to benefit tribal peoples. Fürer-Haimendorf attributed this success to the political pressure put on local government officials by Banjara leaders and their allies in the ruling party. Thus, the Banjaras became, he wrote, "the most privileged community in the district."[64] They were not added to the list of tribes in the adjoining state of Maharashtra. Numbers of them, therefore, migrated in order to access the various programs and land rights available to them in Andhra Pradesh.

Struggling to Be a Tribe: A Political Agitation in Contemporary India

The 1935 Government of India Act, which granted a limited representative government in much of British India, also "reserved" certain constituencies for the "aboriginals." (That English word has now been Indianized by the neologism *adi-vasi*, or "earliest-inhabitant.") Late imperial practice was continued in the constitution of the Indian Republic promulgated in 1950. Specific quotas for "tribes" were allotted in educational institutions and state employment. As the reach of the federal and state governments expanded through the twentieth century, and as rural agriculture became more insecure, demands for recognition as a "tribe" increased. The political and electoral system—supplemented by low-level violence—began to be used to secure opportunities in the state system. Even supposedly anti-state revolutionary movements like the Maoist insurgency often demanded shares in the system, not its destruction. That could mean recognition as "tribes." Thus, Maoists kidnapped a senior government functionary (a District Collector) in 2011. He was released on the promise that two communities— the Konda Reddy and Nooka Dora—should be added to the list of "Scheduled Tribes."[65] Recognition by the state has created a small urban Adivasi middle class whose existence energized other communities' claims to entry. Among other organizable communities "not yet officially listed as S[cheduled] T[ribes], elite political activity consists of trying to make claims to that status."[66]

Some efforts at recognition as a tribe were stymied by strong political counterpressure. In 2007, the Gurjjar community in North India began an agitation demanding that they be classified as a "Scheduled Tribe" by the state government of Rajasthan. They blocked the highways leading to the Indian capital, New Delhi, and also obstructed major railway lines for several days. A clash between a crowd of Gurjjars and the police resulted in the police firing and the death of several people. The Gurjjar leaders were invited to negotiate and demanded a judicial investigation of their claim, declaring that an earlier inquiry from 1981 had been biased. Three months later, the panel headed by a High Court judge also rejected their demand. It reiterated the evaluation made in 1981.That earlier note read in part:

> Regarding Gurjjars, these people are basically milk-sellers and keep cattle. They are fairly well-off and suffer from no shyness of contact with people of other castes. Also, they do not have any primitive traits [for them] to be considered for inclusion in ST list.

The reader will perceive how colonial stereotypes were invoked in this instance. But there was more than colonial discourse at work. There was also serious political pressure on the state government as well as the central one. The major beneficiaries of tribal status in Rajasthan had been another powerful and militant rural community, the Meenas. They had achieved "tribal" status under colonial rule, perhaps because some were deemed animists, some labeled Hindu, and some Muslim. Such transgression of the sharp boundaries of colonial ethnology required a distinct label. Sections of them were then proclaimed to be a criminal tribe under section 5 of Act XXVII of 1871 in the Gurgaon District of the Punjab and were also proclaimed and registered in the following states of the Rajputana: Jodhpur, Bikaner, Sirohi, Kishengarh, and Bharatpur.[67]

Having achieved tribal status in colonial times, Meenas were added to the list of "Scheduled Tribes" eligible for affirmative action under the Republic of India. When the Gurjjars began to demand admission to that status, Meenas realized that any extension of "Scheduled Tribe" status would dilute their own benefits. Crowds of Gurjjars blocked major railway lines and roads again in 2008, with twenty-two of them being killed in police firing.

Meenas then opposed the Gurjjars' being given the status of a Scheduled Tribe by political agitation and also with threats of violence. Isolated Gurjjar villages were besieged by crowds of armed Meenas. A reporter interviewed one resident by phone. This is what he heard:

> There are two trucks with soldiers inside that keep coming in and going out of the village but we are all scared. The Meenas have blocked the road and are not allowing anyone in or out and are harassing the Gurjjars who dare to venture out. I haven't seen my neighbour since Friday night because all Gurjjar families have locked themselves in.[68]

It became an issue in the election campaign of 2019. Having received the Gurjjars' support, the newly elected state government finally passed a law granting Gurjjars and four other communities a 5 percent quota in government employment and educational institutions, without reducing the percentage for other communities.

In this episode, neither the aspirants to tribal status nor the recognized tribes showed any of the "shyness" or timidity elsewhere deemed a necessary feature of aboriginality. The process of tribal recognition that began as an artifact of colonial political ethnology had simply become a regular part of the turbulent Indian democratic process.

State institutions and the political system thus threw theoretical consistency to the winds in order to work out a reallocation of real and symbolic resources to pacify a newly emerged and turbulent constituency which had the capacity to paralyze communications throughout the region and around the national capital of New Delhi. Tribal identities were always political processes.

Chapter Conclusion

This chapter has introduced the reader to the many varieties of tribes in Asian history. Some no longer exist, like the Turkish-speaking nomads who made Anatolia Turkish. Some have been re-molded by powerful bureaucracies as in the People's Republic of China. Some persist and have adapted to the modern state and seek recognition as Indigenous Peoples in the New World Order. Some maintain an insurgent presence, and some have but recently invented themselves as tribes.

Conclusion

"There are nine and sixty ways
Of constructing tribal lays..."

— Rudyard Kipling, 1891

I hope the reader will permit me an extended metaphor for the peoples and processes that I have delineated in dry and prosaic terms throughout the preceding pages. The orbit of our planet ensures that we have seasons of snow. Each snowflake, like each life, is unique. Billions of them fall each year. If the snows do not melt, but accumulate, the lowest layers are slowly squeezed into strata of hard ice until the pressure forces them to flow away as glaciers. During the last Ice Age, such glaciers advanced irresistibly over the earth, grinding across the land, wearing down the mountains, carrying rocks and boulders far from their native bedrock, and pushing far out across frozen seas. Then the glaciers began to retreat. The sea ice thawed: retreating glaciers flowed away as rivers, withdrew into high mountain valleys, melted into great lakes, and disintegrated as icebergs—floating mountains still deadly for ships. But even in the depths of the Ice Age, there were limits to the advance of glaciers—there were always lands too dry or too hot for them to advance there.

We have witnessed the similar advances and retreats of empires across the earth in the past four thousand years. And empires have met their limits too: the forests of Amazonia for the Incas, the arid prairie of the American Southwest for the Aztecs, the ocean of grass across Eurasia, from the Black Sea to the Sea of Japan, for the Chinese, Persians, Greeks, and Arabs. In South and Southeast Asia, they were slowed or stopped by woodlands, natural and manmade. There are still poor and rugged valleys—from Albania, Montenegro, Daghestan, and Kurdistan, to Afghanistan, Nagaland, Mizoram, the 'Golden Triangle' and beyond—that empires and successor states find hard to dominate. Throughout history, all these places harbored recalcitrant communities, peoples who, as Morton Fried pointed out, formed themselves into defensive and offensive organizations, created perhaps for protection, but well-suited to predation. Around 1900, it may have seemed that these were all relics of the past, likely to disappear as soon as the great empires triturated human societies into uniformity.

All these imperial projects failed by the beginning of the twenty-first century. An important retreat began at the end of World War II in 1945, and a second phase began with the collapse of the Soviet Union in 1992. Soon after the seemingly successful US-led NATO invasion of Afghanistan, Niall Ferguson, a Harvard historian wrote a book suggesting the United States establish another empire to succeed the British. That project did not get far. The outcome of the PRC's current imperial project is still uncertain.

Meanwhile, chunks of relic empire, left behind like the snows of Kilimanjaro, have sought to refashion themselves into national states. Some of these—notably Russia—resemble the old empires, and many, as an Egyptian diplomat said, have become "tribes with flags" (and now, UN memberships). But, as we have seen in chapter 4, empires often began as merely tribes with flags. Broken empires also left new tribes across the landscape. In politically difficult times, these fragments might regrow with new names and new chiefs.

On the other hand, signs of a new advance of empires are not entirely absent in the twenty-first century, even if the American venture in Iraq and Afghanistan has misfired. But as I indicated in the introduction to this volume, a resurgence of tribes is also to be seen. Where the state is strong and growing—as in the People's Republic of China—"tribes" have been recognized, but also disciplined and sorted into "minority nationalities," at least for the moment.

The rugged uplands of the Southeast Asian mountain massif still retain recalcitrant social organizations and tribes, Liberation Armies and National Socialist Councils. Where the state is politically decentralized, as in the Republic of India, the "tribe" as a legal and political category was demarcated in British imperial times but has been transformed by new powerful sociopolitical processes in a stably chaotic society. Northwest of India, the former tribal heartland of the Afghan-Pakistani border has moved back toward tribalism anew. The Inner Asian lands from which the Soviet Empire retreated are once more ruled by strongmen with large retinues. Historically, that was how tribes began and how tribal empires were founded. It is not inconceivable that these processes may recur. The nation-state as political organization is but two centuries old, and many of the newer ones are fraying at the edges. Empires are older political forms, but they are generally in retreat. Are tribes destined to disappear like the empires they resisted and the empires they founded? As Sam Goldwyn said, prediction is hard, especially the future. But I would say that as long as states are fragile and failing, the tribe as an intermediate organization cannot entirely vanish from the earth.

This book has ended by surveying the many types of political organizations recognized as tribes in today's Asia. I hope that the journey through time and distance has equipped the reader with analytic tools to unpack the ways in which the seemingly simple concept of tribe is deployed in political, academic, and popular media discourses of our time.

NOTES

Introduction

[1] Emily Farra, "Which Street Style Tribe Did You Join in 2017?" *Vogue*, December 18, 2017: https://www.vogue.com/article/street-style-tribes-of-2017-top-trends-streetwear-demna-gvasalia-suits.

[2] Clifford Geertz, "The Integrative Revolution: Primordial Sentiments and Civil Politics in the New States," in *Old Societies and New States*, Clifford Geertz, ed. (New York: Free Press 1963), 105–157.

[3] Amy Chua, *Political Tribes: Group Instinct and the Fate of Nations* (Penguin Books, 2018), 164.

[4] A *New York Times* columnist recently accused President Trump of torqueing up "tribal friction and cruelty." Maureen Dowd, "Think Outside the Box Jack: Trump, Twitter and the Society-Crushing Pursuit of Monetized Rage," *New York Times*, June 6, 2020, https://www.nytimes.com/2020/05/30/opinion/sunday/trump-twitter-jack-dorsey.html.

[5] Robert Burns, Lolita C. Baldor, and Matthew Lee, "Trump Defends Decision to Abandon Kurdish Allies in Syria," *AP News*. October 8, 2019. https://www.apnews.com/ac3115b4eb564288a03a5b8be868d2e5.

[6] Donald Horowitz, *Ethnic Groups in Conflict*, 2nd ed. (Berkeley: University of California Press, 2000), xi–xii.

[7] Hussein D. Hassan, *Iraq: Tribal Structure, Social, and Political Activities* (Washington DC: Congressional report, 2007), https://apps.dtic.mil/dtic/tr/fulltext/u2/a464737.pdf. "Tribe" is, of course, not the word currently used in Iraqi Arabic. Hassan translates *ashira* as "tribe" and labels a confederation of such tribes as a *qabila*.

[8] Roberto T. Gonzales, "Going 'Tribal': Notes on Pacification in the 21st Century," *Anthropology Today*, 25, no. 2 (Apr. 2009): 15–19.

[9] Cited in Sumit Guha, "States, Tribes, Castes: A Historical Re-exploration in Comparative Perspective," Special Article, *Economic and Political Weekly*, 50, nos. 46–47 (November 2015): 50–57.

[10] Cited in Guha, "States, Tribes, Castes," 50.

[11] Amnesty International, *Pakistan: The Tribal Justice System*. AI Index: ASA 33/024/2002 (2002).

[12] Mandy Sadan, *Being and Becoming Kachin: Histories beyond the State in the Borderworlds of Burma* (Oxford: Oxford University Press, 2013), 10.

[13] Benjamin D. Hopkins, "The Frontier Crimes Regulation and Frontier Governmentality," *Journal of Asian Studies*, 74, no. 2 (2015): 369–389.

[14] Steadman Upham, ed. *The Evolution of Political Systems: Sociopolitics in Small-Scale Sedentary Societies* (Cambridge: Cambridge University Press, 1990), xiv–xvi.

[15] D. M. Bondarenko, Leonid E. Grinin, and Andrey V. Korotayev, "Alternatives of Social Evolution," in *The Early State;* Leonid E. Grinin et al., eds., The Early State, Its Alternatives and Analogues (Volgograd: Uchitel, 2004).

[16] We shall explore many of these trajectories through Asian history in chapter 4.

[17] Hassan, *Iraq*, 3–4.

[18] Wolfram Lacher, "Families, Tribes and Cities in the Libyan Revolution," *Middle East Policy*, no. 4 (Winter 2011): 140–55.

[19] James Scott, *The Art of Not Being Governed: An Anarchist History of Upland Southeast Asia* (New Haven, CT: Yale University Press, 2009), 208–12.

[20] Fredrik Barth, *Political Leadership among Swat Pathans* (London: The Athlone Press, 1959), 133–34.

[21] Karl Wittfogel, *Oriental Despotism: A Comparative Study of Total Power* (New Haven: Yale University Press, 1957), 17. ACLS Humanities Ebook.

[22] S. D. Goitein, *Jews and Arabs: Their Contacts through the Ages* (New York: Schocken Books, 1964 reprint), 14.

[23] Cited in Nicola Di Cosmo, *Ancient China and Its Enemies: The Rise of Nomadic Power in East Asian History* (Cambridge: Cambridge University Press, 2002), 137.

[24] Mountstuart Elphinstone, *An Account of the Kingdom of Caubul and Its Dependencies*, 2 vols. (London: Richard Bentley, 1842), 1:323.

[25] Elphinstone, *Kingdom of Caubul*, 1:323.

[26] John Malcolm, *A Memoir of Central India Including Malwa and Adjoining Provinces; with the History and Copious Illustrations of the Past and Present Condition of That Country*, 2 vols. (New Delhi: Sagar Publications, 1970 reprint): 2: 113–14, 123–24.

[27] T. N. Atre, *Gamv-Gada*, [1915] (Pune: Varda Books, 1989 reprint), 166–69.

[28] Cited in Magnus Fiskesjö, "On the 'Raw' and the 'Cooked' Barbarians of Imperial China," *Inner Asia*, 1, no. 2 (1999), 139–168.

[29] Peter Golden, "Ethnogenesis in the Tribal Zone: The Shaping of the Türks," *Archivum Eurasia Medii Aevi* 16 (2008/2009): 73–112. The Sanskrit political tradition was, as we shall see later in this chapter, more balanced.

[30] Cited in Guha, "States, Tribes, Castes," 53.

[31] Ibn Khaldun, *The Muqaddimah: An Introduction to History*, trans. Franz Rosenthal. 3 vols, 2nd ed. (Princeton: Princeton University Press, 1967) Vol. 1, chapter 2.

[32] Allan J. Fromherz, *Ibn Khaldun: Life and Times* (Edinburgh: University of Edinburgh Press, 2010), 2.

[33] Frank Rosenthal, preface to *The Muqaddimah*, Vol. 1, by Khaldun, lxviii–lxxxvi; Ibn Khaldun, *The Muqaddimah*, 249–254.

[34] Pierre Bourdieu, *Outline of a Theory of Practice,* trans. Richard Nice (Cambridge: Cambridge University Press, 1977).

[35] Fromherz, *Ibn Khaldun*, 65–67, 84–91.

[36] Tapper, "The Tribes in Eighteenth- and Nineteenth-Century Iran," in *The Cambridge History of Iran*, ed. P. Avery, G.R.G. Hambly and C. Melville (Cambridge: Cambridge University Press, 1991), 506–41; Lambton cited, 507.

[37] For the ancient period, see Thomas Trautmann, *Kautilya and the Arthsasastra: A Statistical Investigation of the Authorship and Evolution of the Text* (Leiden: E. J. Brill, 1971), 10–15; Sumit Guha, *Environment and Ethnicity in India, c. 1200–1991* (Cambridge: Cambridge University Press 1999), 150–163. ACLS Humanities Ebook.

Chapter 1

[1] Golden, "Ethnogenesis in the tribal zone", 1, n.2

[2] Morton H. Fried, *The Evolution of Political Society: An Essay in Political Anthropology* (New York: Random House, 1967), 183.

[3] Frank N. Pieke, "Beyond orthodoxy: Social and cultural anthropology in the People's Republic of China," in *Asian Anthropology*, ed. Jan Van Bremen, Eyal Ben-Ari, and Syed Farid Alatas. (London: Routledge, 2004), 59–79; 60. Taylor & Francis eBooks Open Access.

[4] Edmund R. Leach, *The Political Systems of Highland Burma: A Study of Kachin Social Structure* (London: Athlone Press, 1990 reprint), 57–61, 198.

[5] Urgunge Onon, trans. and ed., *The Secret History of the Mongols: The Life and Times of Chinggis Khan* (Abingdon: Routledge Curzon, 2013), 19–25, 279.

[6] Igor de Rachewiltz, "The Secret History of the Mongols," 60. *The Mongolia Society Bulletin*, 9, no. 1 (16) (Spring, 1970): 55–69, emphasis added.

[7] Fredrik Barth, "Pathan Identity and Its Maintenance," in *Ethnic Groups and Boundaries: The Social Organization of Culture Difference*, ed. Fredrik Barth (Boston: Little, Brown and Company, 1969), 13, 117–134. Akbar S. Ahmed, *Millennium and Charisma Among Pathans: A Critical Essay in Social Anthropology* (London: Routledge, 2012 reprint), 78–80.

[8] Elphinstone, *Kingdom of Caubul*, 1:404 and footnotes.

[9] Klaus Ferdinand, *Preliminary Notes on Hazara Culture: The Danish Scientific Mission to Afghanistan, 1953–55*, Historsk-filosofiske Meddelser. Bind 37 nr.5 (Kobenhavn: Munksgaard, 1959), 13–14.

[10] Cited in Guha, *Environment and Ethnicity in India*, 119. Emphasis added.

[11] George W. Forrest, ed., *Selections from the Minutes and Other Official Writings of the Honorable Mountstuart Elphinstone* (London: Richard Bentley, 1884), 448–9 for example.

[12] "Samuel 8:1–2," accessed May 29, 2020, https://www.kingjamesbibleonline.org/1-Samuel-Chapter-8.

[13] Maurice Walshe, trans., *The Long Discourses of the Buddha, a Translation of the Digha Nikaya* (Boston: Wisdom Publications, E-book, 2005), 27:21, 413.

[14] R.C. Majumdar, *Corporate Life in Ancient India,* 3rd ed. (Calcutta: Firma K. L. Mukhopadhyay, 1969), 217–19.

[15] Michael Szonyi, *The Art of Being Governed: Everyday Politics in Late Imperial China* (Princeton: Princeton University Press, 2017), 25–42.

[16] Fiskesjö, "On the 'Raw,'" 151-54 and Notes 60–64.

[17] Anatoly Khazanov, *Nomads and the Outside World*, with a Foreword by Ernest Gellner, trans. Julia Crookenden. 2nd ed. (Madison WI: University of Wisconsin Press, 1994), 50, 95–96.

[18] Nicola Di Cosmo, *Ancient China and its Enemies: The Rise of Nomadic Power in East Asian History* (Cambridge: Cambridge University Press, 2002), 161–3.

[19] Ying-shi Yü, "Han Foreign Relations," in *The Cambridge History of China. Volume 1: The Ch'in and Han Empires, 221 BC–AD 220*, ed. Denis Twitchett and Michael Loewe (Cambridge: Cambridge University Press, 2008 [1986]), 377–462, 384, n.15 https://doi-org.ezproxy.lib.utexas.edu/10.1017/CHOL9780521243278

[20] Yü, "The Hsiung-nu", in *The Cambridge History of Early Inner Asia*, ed. D. Sinor (Cambridge: Cambridge University Press, 1990), 377–462.

[21] Report dated c.1570, cited in Thomas J. Barfield, *Perilous Frontier: Nomadic Empires and China* (Cambridge: Basil Blackwell, 1989), 247.

[22] This paragraph (including quotes) is written from Lin Hang, "Conquer and Govern: The Rise of the Jurchen and Their Jin Dynasty," in *Political Strategies of Identity-Building in Non-Han Empires in China*, ed. Francesca Fiaschetti and Julia Schneider (Wiesbaden: Otto Harrassowitz, 2014), 37–57.

[23] Christopher Atwood, "Notion of Tribe in Medieval China: Ouyang Xiu and the Shatuo Dynastic Myth," in *Miscellanea Asiatica*, edited by Dennis Aigle et al. (Nettetal: Sankt Augustin, 2010), 593–621.

[24] Audrey I. Richards, "A Problem of Anthropological Approach," *Bantu Studies: A Journal Devoted to the Scientific Study of Bantu, Hottentot and Bushman* 15, no. 1 (1941): 45–52, cited in Susan McKinnon, "Domestic Exceptions: Evans-Pritchard and the Creation of Nuer Patrilineality and Equality," *Cultural Anthropology*, 15, no. 1 (Feb., 2000): 35–83, 35.

[25] Cited in Atwood, "Notion of Tribe", 599–600.

[26] Mark C. Elliott, *The Manchu Way: The Eight Banners and Ethnic Identity in Late Imperial China* (Stanford: Stanford University Press, 2001), 196–97; Edward J.M. Rhoads, *Manchus and Han: Ethnic Relations and Political Power in Late Qing and Early Republican China, 1861–1928* (Seattle: University of Washington Press, 2000), 67–70.

[27] Sumit Guha, *History and Collective Memory in South Asia, 1200–2000* (Seattle: University of Washington Press, 2019), 40–47.

[28] Pamela K. Crossley, "Making Mongols," in *Empire at the Margins: Culture, Ethnicity, and Frontier in Early Modern China,* ed. Pamela Crossley, Helen F. Siu, and Donald S. Sutton (Berkerley: University of California Press, 2006), 58–82.

[29] Christopher P. Atwood, ed., *Encyclopedia of Mongolia and the Mongol Empire* (New York: Facts on File, 2004), 602–612.

[30] Atwood, *Encyclopedia,* 18–19; Barfield, *The Perilous Frontier,* 212–221.

[31] Lhamsuren Munkh-Erdene, "Where Did the Mongol Empire Come From? Medieval Mongol Ideas of People, State and Empire," *Inner Asia,* 13, no. 2 (2011), 216.

[32] Ernest Gellner, foreword to *Nomads,* by Khazanov, xv.

[33] Charles J. Halperin, "*Tsarev ulus*: Russia in the Golden Horde," *Cahiers du monde russe et soviétique,* 23, no 2, (1982), 257–63.

[34] Richard Tapper, "The Tribes in Eighteenth- and Nineteenth-Century Iran" in *The Cambridge History of Iran,* Vol. 7 (Cambridge: Cambridge University Press, 1991), 506–541, esp. 506-7.

[35] Ferdinand, *Preliminary Notes on Hazara Culture,* 22.

[36] Hassan, *Iraq,* passim.

[37] I have consulted the Sanskrit text in R.P. Kangle ed. *Kauṭilīya Arthaśāstra* (Delhi: Motilal Banarsidas, 1999). For a modern annotated translation, see Patrick Olivelle, *King, Governance and Law in Ancient India: Kauṭilya's Arthaśāstra* (South Asian Edition. New Delhi: Oxford University Press, 2013). This background is taken from the Introduction, 1–38.

[38] Sumit Guha, *Beyond Caste: Identity and Power in South Asia, Past and Present* (Leiden: Brill, 2013), 157.

[39] Ann G. Gold and Bhojuram Gujar, *In the Time of Trees and Sorrows* (Durham NC: Duke University Press, 2002), 214–20.

[40] Majumdar, *Corporate Life,* 244–49, 256–59.

[41] Abu'l Fazl. *The Ain-i-Akbari of Abul-Fazl-i-Allami.* Translated by H.S. Jarrett, revised by Jadunath Sarkar, Vol. II (Calcutta: Royal Asiatic Society, 1949); G.H. Khare, ed., *Persian Sources of Maratha History,* Vol. 6 (Pune: Bharat Itihas Samshodhak Mandal, 1973), 3–5.

[42] Ahsan Raza Khan, *Chieftains in the Mughal Empire* (Simla: Indian Institute of Advanced Study, 1977), 2–11.

[43] Maran La Raw, "On the continuing relevance of E.R. Leach's *Political Systems of Highland Burma* to Kachin studies," in *Social Dynamics in the Highlands of Southeast Asia: Reconsidering Political Systems of Highland Burma* by E.R. Leach, ed. F. Robinne and M. Sadan (Leiden: Brill, 2007), 31–66; Mandy Sadan "Translating Gumlau: History, the Kachin and Edmund Leach," in *Social Dynamics in the Highlands,* 67–90.

[44] Leach, *Political Systems,* 213–226.

[45] Jean Michaud, *Historical Dictionary of the Peoples of the Southeast Asian Massif* (Lanham Md.: Scarecrow Press, 2006), 89–90, 171–2, 204–5.

[46] Leach, *Political Systems*, 197–199

[47] Stanley J. Tambiah, "The Galactic Polity: The Structure of Traditional Kingdoms in Southeast Asia," *Annals of the New York Academy of Sciences* 293, no. 1 (1977): 69–97.

[48] Geoffrey Benjamin, "On Being Tribal in the Malay World," in *Tribal Communities in the Malay World: Historical, Social and Cultural Perspectives*, ed. Cynthia Chou and Geoffrey Benjamin (Singapore: Institute of Southeast Asian Studies, 2001), 7–76. I am indebted to L.J. Bulten for this reference.

Chapter 2

[1] *A Latin Dictionary*, online http://www.perseus.tufts.edu/hopper/text?doc=Perseu s:text:1999.04.0059:entry=tribus; and Robert Ainsworth *Thesaurus Lingvae Latinae* at https://play.google.com/store/books/details?id=rzZLAAAAcAAJ&rdid=book-rzZLAAAAcAAJ&rdot=1.

[2] Luís de Matos, ed., *Imagens do Oriente no século XVI* (Lisboa: Imprensa Nacional—Casa de Moeda, 1985) for many sixteenth-century examples.

[3] This section up to this point is based on Guha, *Beyond Caste*, 19–44.

[4] Elphinstone, *Kingdom of Caubul*, 1:210–211.

[5] Elphinstone 1, Kingdom of Caubul, 1:214, emphasis added; C. A. Bayly, *Elphinstone, Mountstuart (1779–1859), Oxford Dictionary of National Biography*. DNB onlinehttps://doi.org/10.1093/ref:odnb/8752.

[6] Ferdinand, Preliminary Notes on Hazara Culture, 13–14.

[7] So wrote Jean Nicot, *Thresoir de la Langue Francais* (1606) via ARTFL (my translation). The 1798 Dictionary of the Academie Francaise described *tribu* as an ancient form among the Greeks and Romans, but added that it was also found as a subdivision in some large nations like the Tartars. Accessed Feb. 29, 2020, https://artflsrv03-uchicago-edu.ezproxy. lib.utexas.edu/philologic4/publicdicos/query?report=bibliography&head=tribu.

[8] François Martin, *Mémoires de François Martin*, Vol. 2 (Paris: Societe de l'Histoire des Colonies Francaises, 1934), 325.

[9] "Discourse", 1804 in *Miscellaneous Works of the Right Honourable Sir James Mackintosh*, ed. Robert James Mackintosh, Single volume edition (London: Longman, 1851), 535-6, 535–541.

[10] Moreau de Jonnès, "Recherches historiques sur les Caraïbes," *Journal des voyages, découvertes et navigations modernes* 2, no. 5 (1819), 5–27; J. Rehmann and M. Frièville, "État politique et militaire des Khalkas-Mongols," *Journal des voyages, découvertes et navigations modernes*, 2, no. 5 (1819), 27–51, cited p. 30; *Revue des Deux Mondes*.

[11] François Ducuing, "La Guerre de Montagne II: La Kabylie. Marechal Bugeaud, *Revue des Deux Mondes* (1829–1971), *Nouvelle Période*, 10, no. 2 (15 AVRIL 1851), 225–274.

[12] Arabe, kabaïlyy (le 2nd a avec un accent long), adjectif tiré de kabail [adjective derived from kabail] (2nd a: a long), [plural form of kabilat, rendered in French as] *tribu, famille, peuplade berbère*, "tribe, family, Berber people." https://dvlf-uchicago-edu.ezproxy.lib. utexas.edu/mot/kabyle.

[13] Charles F. Keyes, "Presidential Address: 'The Peoples of Asia'—Science and Politics in the Classification of Ethnic Groups in Thailand, China, and Vietnam," *Journal of Asian Studies* 61, no. 4 (2002), 1163–1204, cited 1169 f.n. 12.

[14] Henri Maître, *Les régions Moï du Sud indo-chinois: le plateau du Darlac* (Paris: Plon, 1909), 157.

[15] Oscar Salemink, *The Ethnography of Vietnam's Central Highlanders: A Historical Contextualization 1850–1970* (London: Routledge Curzon, 2003), 60–62.

[16] In the French Empire, these were labeled *évolués* or *évoluées*—"evolved" or "sophisticated" ones.

[17] All evidence in this section is taken from Sumit Guha, "Lower Strata, Older Races and Aboriginal Peoples: Racial Anthropology and Mythic History Past and Present," *Journal of Asian Studies* 57, no. 2 (1998), 423–441.

[18] J. Celériér, "Chez Berbéres du Maroc," *Annales d'Histoire Economique et Sociale* T.8, No. 39 (1936), 209–211, 217.

[19] Cited in Guha, *Environment and Ethnicity*, 19. Emphasis added. The narrative is identical to that suggested by Frere eighty years earlier.

[20] Megan Moodie, *We Were Adivasis: Aspiration in an Indian Scheduled Tribe* (Chicago: University of Chicago Press, 2015), 35–42, especially "A Brief Note on 'Tribe' in the Indian Context."

[21] Frank Dikötter, "The Racialization of the Globe: An Interactive Interpretation," *Ethnic and Racial Studies* 31, no. 8 (2008), 1478–1496.

[22] Elman R. Service, "The Mind of Lewis H. Morgan [and Comments and Reply]," *Current Anthropology*, 22, no. 1 (Feb. 1981), 25–43.

[23] Eleanor Kingwell-Banham and Dorian Q. Fuller, "Shifting Cultivators in South Asia: Expansion, Marginalisation and Specialization," *Quaternary International* 249 (2012), 84–95.

[24] Cited in Sumit Guha, "Forest Polities and Agrarian Empires: The Khandesh Bhils c. 1700–1850," *Indian Economic and Social History Review* 33, no. 2 (1996), 133–153; quote on pp. 133–34.

[25] Guha, *Environment and Ethnicity*, 10–29.

[26] Gananath Obeyesekere, "Colonial Histories and Vädda Primitivism: An Unorthodox Reading of Kandy Period Texts," accessed September 4, 2020. www.artsrilanka.org/essays/ vaddaprimitivism/index.html. I owe this valuable reference to L. J. Bulten.

[27] Robert Nichols, ed., *The Frontier Crimes Regulation: A History in Documents* (Karachi: Oxford University Press, 2013), Editorial Introduction x–xvii; text 157–161.

[28] Hopkins, "The Frontier Crimes Regulation and Frontier Governmentality," 369–389 and Benjamin D. Hopkins, *Ruling the Savage Periphery: Frontier Governance and the Making of the Modern State* (Cambridge MA: Harvard University Press, 2020), 10–29.

[29] Meena Radhakrishna, *Dishonoured by History: "Criminal Tribes" and British Colonial Policy* (Hyderabad: Orient Longman, 2001), 27–45.

[30] Cited in Guha, *Beyond Caste*, 199–200.

[31] Guha, *Environment and Ethnicity*, 182–198.

[32] Leach, *Political System of Highland Burma*, 55–57.

[33] Dikötter, "Racialization," 1488–1489.

[34] Pieke, "Beyond Orthodoxy," 69.

[35] Obeyesekere, "Colonial Histories."

[36] Citations in Guha, *Environment and Ethnicity*, 4–6, except John R. Wood, "India's Narmada River Dams: Sardar Sarovar under Siege," *Asian Survey* 33, no. 10 (Oct. 1993): 968–984, quote, 975.

Chapter 3

[1] Ian Scoones, "New Ecology and the Social Sciences: What Prospects for a Fruitful Engagement?" *Annual Review of Anthropology* 28 (1999): 479–507.

[2] James C. Scott, *Art of Not Being Governed: An Anarchist History of Upland Southeast Asia* (New Haven: Yale University Press, 2009).

[3] James C. Scott, *Against the Grain: A Deep History of the Earliest States* (New Haven: Yale University Press, 2017).

[4] Yü, Y, "The Hsiung-nu," 122.

[5] Ibn Khaldun, *Muqaddimah*, 1: 249.

[6] Fromherz, *Ibn Khaldun: Life and Times*, 141–142.

[7] Tapper, "The Tribes," 7: 506–541.

[8] Karl Wittfogel, *Oriental Despotism*, 17.

[9] A. M. Khazanov, *Nomads and the Outside World*, 40-63.

[10] Khazanov, *Nomads and the Outside World*, xiii–xvi, 132–135.

[11] Rudi P. Lindner, *Nomads and Ottomans in Medieval Anatolia* (Bloomington: Research Institute for Inner Asian Studies, 1983), 9.

[12] A. M. Khazanov, "Nomads of the Eurasian Steppes in Historical Retrospective," in *The Early State*, 476–500.

[13] Tapper, *Frontier Nomads*, 286.

[14] Barfield, Perilous Frontier, 16–30.

[15] Di Cosmo *Ancient China*, 44–57. Yü, "The Hsiung-nu," 118–21. This connects with Khazanov's suggestion that militarized nomadism took shape in the west central steppes and diffused eastward.

[16] Di Cosmo, *Ancient China*, 77–90, 124–131.

[17] Barfield, *Perilous Frontier*, 100–110 provides the most sophisticated model of such organizations.

[18] Khazanov, "Myths and Paradoxes of Nomadism," *European Journal of Sociology* 22, no.1 (1981): 141–53.

[19] Barfield, *Perilous Frontier,* 1–31.

[20] Barfield, *Perilous Frontier*, 220. He states that there were only one million Mongols in Khubilai Khan's domains in 1290, versus ten million Chinese subjects in North China and sixty million in the south.

[21] Di Cosmo, *Ancient China*, 268–286; Timothy May, "Mongol Warfare in the Pre-Dissolution Period," *Golden Horde Review*, No. 2 (2015), 7–19.

[22] Khazanov, "Nomads in the History of the Sedentary World," in *Nomads in the Sedentary World*, ed. A.M. Khazanov and André Wink (Richmond: Curzon, 2001), 16–18.

[23] Atwood, *Encyclopedia*, 604–605.

[24] John Masson Smith, "Ayn Jalout" *Harvard Journal of Asiatic Studies* 44, no. 2 (Dec. 1984): 307–345; Di Cosmo, *Ancient China,* 178–180.

[25] Yucheng Yü, "The Hsiung-nu," 130–131.

[26] Barfield, *The Perilous Frontier*, 5–12.

[27] Peter Golden, *An Introduction to the History of the Turkic Peoples: Ethnogenesis and State Formation in Medieval and Early Modern Eurasia and the Middle East* (Wiesbaden: Otto Harrassowitz, 1992); for numbers, p.162, f.n. 38.

[28] Lindner, *Nomads and Ottomans, passim.*

[29] Richard Tapper, *Frontier Nomads of Iran: A Political History of the Shahsevan* (Cambridge: Cambridge University Press, 1997), 114, 284-87.

[30] Fredrik Barth, "The System of Social Stratification in Swat" in *Aspects of Caste in South India, Ceylon and North-West Pakistan* , ed. Edmund Leach (Cambridge: Cambridge University Press, 1960), 113–146.

[31] Fredrik Barth, "Ecologic Relationships of Ethnic Groups in Swat, North Pakistan," *American Anthropologist, New Series,* 58, no. 6 (Dec. 1956): 1079–1089.

[32] This paragraph is based on Guha, *Environment and Ethnicity*, 50–51.

[33] Wheeler M. Thackston, trans., ed., and annotated, *The Baburnama: Memoirs of Babur, Prince and Emperor* (New York: The Modern Library, 2002), 331–335.

[34] Guha, *Environment and Ethnicity*, 139–142.

[35] All evidence in this section is taken from Guha, *Environment and Ethnicity*, 108–149.

[36] Leach, *Political Systems*, 30.

[37] Leach, *Political Systems*, 237–245.

[38] Scott, *The Art of Not Being Governed, passim*, 207–208.

[39] Michaud, *Historical Dictionary*, 204–205; emphasis in the original.

Chapter 4

[1] Barfield, *Perilous Frontier*, 229–263; Pamela Crossley, *A Translucent Mirror: History and Identity in Qing Imperial Ideology* (Berkeley: University of California Press, 1999), 177-215

[2] This account is largely based on Golden, *Turkic Peoples*, 3–28, 161–163, and *passim*; Barfield, *Perilous Frontier*, 151–155.

[3] Lindner, *Nomads and Ottomans* 32–35.

[4] Lindner, *Nomads and Ottomans*, passim, and viii. This section draws relies almost entirely on Lindner's work.

[5] Nicola Di Cosmo, Allen J. Frank, and Peter B. Golden, eds., *The Cambridge History of Inner Asia: The Chinggisid Age* [henceforth *CHIA*]. (Cambridge: Cambridge University Press, 2009), Introduction, 1–6.

[6] Michael Szonyi, *Practicing Kinship: Lineage and Descent in Late Imperial China* (Stanford: Stanford University Press, 2002), 98–102.

[7] Peter B. Golden, "Inner Asia c. 1200," in *CHIA*, 9–25.

[8] Such explosive growth has analogies elsewhere. Pekka Hamalainen, *The Comanche Empire* (New Haven: Yale University Press, 2008) details how a few small bands of Native Americans who originally hunted on foot coalesced into the powerful Comanche tribe within a few decades of becoming horsemen. Their horse-based dominance of a large tract of Southwest America baffled three European powers for half a century.

[9] Peter Jackson, "The Mongol Age in Eastern Inner Asia," in *CHIA*, 26–28.

[10] Barfield, *Perilous Frontier*, 220–221.

[11] Atwood, "Banner, Otog, Thousand: Appanage Communities as the Basic Unit of Traditional Mongolian Society," *Mongolian Studies*, 34 (2012), 1–75. But see Gellner, foreword to *Nomads* by Khazanov, xv.

[12] This paragraph is drawn from Crossley, *Translucent Mirror*, 311–315.

[13] Abolala Soudavar, "The Early Safavids and Their Cultural Interactions With Surrounding States," in *Iran and the Surrounding World*, ed. Nikki R. Kedie and Rudi Matthee (Seattle: University of Washington Press, 2002), 90-91; Tapper, *Frontier Nomads*, 47–49.

[14] Sussan Babaie, Kathryn Babayan, Ina Baghdadiantz, and Massumeh Farhad, *Slaves of the Shah: New Elites of Safavid Iran* (London: I. B. Tauris, 2004), 1–48.

[15] Tapper, *Frontier Nomads*, 55, 217–280.

[16] Ataollah Hassani, "Names and Appellations in the Shahsevan-e Baghdadi Confederacy," *Nomadic Peoples, New Series*, 7, no. 2, Special Issue: Nomads and Nomadism in Post-revolutionary Iran (2003), 48–61.

[17] Yuri Bregel, "Uzbeks, Qazaqs and Turkmen," in *CHIA*, 221–236.

[18] Scott Levi, "Turks and Tajiks in Central Asian History," in *Everyday Life in Central Asia: Past and Present,* ed. Jeff Sahadeo and Russell Zanca (Bloomington: Indiana University Press, 2007), 15–31.

[19] This paragraph is drawn from Carter V. Findlay, *The Turks in World History* (New York: Oxford University Press, 2005), 148–149.

[20] Adrienne Edgar, "Everyday Life among the Turkmen Nomads," in *Everyday Life in Central Asia*, 37–44.

[21] Findlay, *The Turks*, 180–183.

[22] Atwood, *Encyclopedia*. Entries for "Hazara," 215–216, and "Qara'una," 447–448.

[23] M. Hassan Kakar, *A Political and Diplomatic History of Afghanistan* (Leiden: Brill, 2006), 125–138.

[24] Ferdinand, *Preliminary Notes on Hazara Culture*, quoted, 13.

[25] Pamela K. Crossley, *In a Translucent Mirror*, 74–82. The section on the Manchus has benefited from email communication with Professor Crossley, October 2019. I remain responsible for errors and overstatements.

[26] Crossley, *Translucent Mirror*, 99–103.

[27] Crossley, *Translucent Mirror*, 1–134.

[28] Perdue, *China Marches West: The Qing Conquest of Central Eurasia* (Cambridge: Belknap Press of Harvard University Press, 2005), Chapter 8 and 9, 303 ff.

[29] Perdue, *China Marches West*, 332.

[30] Pamela Crossley, *The Manchus* (Oxford: Blackwell Publishing, 1997), 78–101.

[31] These paragraphs are based on Crossley, *Translucent Mirror*, 286–290.

[32] Rhoads, *Manchus and Han*, 67–70.

[33] This discussion is based on Crossley, *Translucent Mirror*, 311–16, and Crossley, "Making Mongols," in *Empire at the Margins*, 58–82.

[34] David Faure, "The Yao Wars in the Mid-Ming and Their Impact on Yao Ethnicity," in *Empire at the Margins*, 171–189, quote 185.

[35] Michael Szonyi, *The Art of Being Governed*, 207–208 for the invention of a lineage founder for registration purposes.

[36] Michael Szonyi, *Practicing Kinship*, 200.

[37] These paragraphs draw heavily from Frank Dikötter, "The Racialization of the Globe," 1478–1496.

[38] Dikötter, "Racialization," 1484.

[39] Thomas S. Mullaney, *Coming to Terms with the Nation: Ethnic Classification in Modern China* (Berkeley: University of California Press, 2011), 92–119. https://hdl-handle-net.ezproxy.lib.utexas.edu/2027/heb.33882.

[40] "The Nation," accessed September 24, 2019. https://www.marxists.org/reference/archive/stalin/works/1913/03a.htm#s1.

[41] "Marxism and the Problem of Linguistics," accessed September 24, 2019, https://www.marxists.org/reference/archive/stalin/works/1950/jun/20.htm.

[42] Mullaney, *Coming to Terms with the Nation*, Table 9, 82.

[43] Wing-hoi Chan, "Ethnic Labels in a Mountainous Region: The Case of She 'Bandits,'" in *Empire at the Margins*, 255–257, *passim*; Pieke "Beyond Orthodoxy," n. 18, 76.

[44] Jean Michaud, Sarah Turner, and Yann Roche, "Mapping Ethnic Diversity in Highland North Vietnam," *Geojournal* 57 (2002): 281–299.

[45] Indrani Chatterjee, *Forgotten Friends: Monks, Marriages, and Memories of Northeast India*. (Delhi: Oxford University Press, 2013).

[46] B. G. Verghese, *India's Northeast Resurgent: Ethnicity, Insurgency, Governance and Development* (New Delhi: Konark Publishers for the Centre for Policy Research, 1996).

[47] https://www.thehindu.com/news/national/other-states/no-extortion-only-legitimate-taxes-levied-nscn-im/article31937480.ece Downloaded September 13, 2020

[48] Brian Beary, ed., *Separatist Movements: A Global Reference* (Washington DC: CQ Press, 2011), 26–30; Michaud, *Historical Dictionary*, 212–214 and 118–120.

[49] Prasit Leepracha, "Becoming Indigenous Peoples in Thailand," *Journal of Southeast Asian Studies*, 50, no. 1 (February 2019), 32–50.

[50] Barth, *Political Leadership*, 10–17, 64–65, 87; "System of Social Stratification in Swat," 113–146, *passim*.

[51] The concept of territorially dominant castes was elaborated by M.N. Srinivas, "Caste in Modern India," *The Journal of Asian Studies*, 16, no. 4 (Aug., 1957), 529–548.

[52] Elphinstone, *Kingdom of Caubul*. 1:201, note.

[53] William H. Tone, *Some Particular Institutions of the Maratta People* (London: Reprinted for J. Derrett, 1799), 29; Jos Gommans, *The Rise of Indo-Afghan Empire, c. 1710–1780* (Delhi: Oxford University Press, 1999), 132–35, 113–120.

[54] S.M. Moens, *Report on the Settlement of the Bareilly District, North-Western Provinces* (Allahabad: North-Western Provinces Government Press, 1874), 29–37, 130–133.

[55] Bernard Cohn, cited in Guha, *History and Collective Memory*, 66.

[56] Cited in Guha, *Environment and Ethnicity*, 171.

[57] Census of India, 1961, B.K. Roy-Burman, *The Siddis: An Ethnographic Study*. (Delhi: Manager of Publications, 1969), 1.

[58] Nandini Sundar, ed., *The Scheduled Tribes and Their India: Politics, Identities, Policies and Work*. (Delhi: Oxford University Press, 2016), Introduction, 1–16.

[59] *Baburnama*, 178–179.

[60] Forsyth, *Highlands of Central India*, 107–108; for Briggs see note 62.

[61] *Selections from the Satara Raja's and Peshwa Diaries*, 8 Parts. (Poona: Deccan Vernacular Translation Society, 1902–1911), Part 1, 183–184.

[62] This section draws heavily from John Briggs, "Account of the Origin, History and Manners of the Race of Men called Bunjaras," in *Transactions of the Literary Society of Bombay*, vol. 1 [1819]. (Reprinted with new pagination, Bombay: Bombay at the Education Society's Press, 1877), 174–197.

[63] Guha, *Environment and Ethnicity,* 122–129.

[64] Christoph von Fürer-Haimendorf, *Tribes of India: The Struggle for Survival* (Berkeley: University of California Press, 1982), 197–198.

[65] Sundar, *The Scheduled Tribes,* 6.

[66] Sundar, *The Scheduled Tribes,* 4.

[67] G. W. Gayer, *Lectures on Some Criminal Tribes of India* and *Religious Mendicants* (Nagpur: Publisher n/a, 1910). https://archive.org/stream/lecturesonsomecr00gayeuoft/lecturesonsomecr00gayeuoft_djvu.txt, for the earlier administrative history of the Meenas.

[68] Pranab Dhal Samanta, "3 Months and a Judge's Panel Make Gurjjars Climb Down," *Indian Express,* June 05, 2007, http://archive.indianexpress.com/news/3-months-and-a-judges-panel-make-gurjjars-climb-down/32764; "Rajasthan Assembly Passes Quota Bill, Gujjars Call Off Stir." *India Today.* February 13, 2019, https://www.indiatoday.in/india/story/rajasthan-government-five-per-cent-quota-bill-gujjars-four-castes-1455070-2019-02-13.

WORKS CITED

Abu'l Fazl-i Allami. *The Ain-i-Akbari of Abul-Fazl-i-Allami*. Translated by H. S. Jarrett, revised by Jadunath Sarkar. Vol. II. Calcutta: Royal Asiatic Society, 1949.

Ahmed, Akbar S. *Millennium and Charisma among Pathans: A Critical Essay in Social Anthropology*. London: Routledge & Kegan Paul, 1976. Reprint, London: Routledge, 2012.

Ainsworth, Robert. "Tribus." *Thesaurus Lingvae Latinae*. London: Mount, 1752. https://play.google.com/store/books/details?id=rzZLAAAAcAAJ&rdid=book-rzZLAAAAcAAJ&rdot=1.

Amnesty International. *Pakistan: The Tribal Justice System*. AI Index: ASA 33/024/2002 (2002). https://www.amnesty.org/en/documents/ASA33/024/2002/en/.

Arthashastra. The Kauṭilīya Arthaśāstra. Part I. Sanskrit Text with a Glossary. Edited by R.P. Kangle. Delhi: Motilal Banarsidass, 1986. Reprint, Delhi: Motilal Banarsidass, 1997.

Atre, Trimbaka Narayana. *Gamv-Gada*. 1915. Reprint, Pune: Varda Books, 1989.

Atwood, Christopher P., ed. *Encyclopedia of Mongolia and the Mongol Empire*. New York: Facts on File, 2004.

———. "The Notion of Tribe in Medieval China: Ouyang Xiu and the Shatuo Dynastic Myth." In *Miscellanea Asiatica*, edited by Dennis Aigle et al., 593–621. Nettetal: Sankt Augustin, 2010.

———. "Banner, Otog, Thousand: Appanage Communities as the Basic Unit of Traditional Mongolian Society." *Mongolian Studies* 34 (2012): 1–75.

Babaie, Susan, Kathryn Babayan, Ina Baghdadiantz-McCabe, and Massumeh Farhad. *Slaves of the Shah: New Elites of Safavid Iran*. London: I. B. Tauris, 2004.

Babur, Zahiruddin Muhammad. *Baburnama: Memoirs of Babur, Prince and Emperor*. Translated by Wheeler M. Thackston. New York: The Modern Library, 2002.

Barfield, Thomas Jefferson. *The Perilous Frontier: Nomadic Empires and China.* Cambridge, MA: Basil Blackwell, 1989.

Barth, Fredrik. "Ecologic Relationships of Ethnic Groups in Swat, North Pakistan." *American Anthropologist, New Series* 58, no. 6 (December 1956): 1079–1089.

———. *Political Leadership among Swat Pathans.* London: The Athlone Press, 1959.

———. ed. *Ethnic Groups and Boundaries: The Social Organization of Culture Difference.* London: George Allen & Unwin, 1969. Reprint, Long Grove: Waveland Press, 1998.

———. "The System of Social Stratification in Swat," in *Aspects of Caste in South India, Ceylon and North-West Pakistan*, edited by Edmund Leach, 113–146. Cambridge: Cambridge University Press, 1960.

Bayly, C. A. "Elphinstone, Mountstuart." *Oxford Dictionary of National Biography.* https://doi.org/10.1093/ref:odnb/8752.

Beary, Brian, ed. *Separatist Movements: A Global Reference.* Washington DC: CQ Press, 2011.

Benjamin, Geoffrey. "On Being Tribal in the Malay World." In *Tribal Communities in the Malay World: Historical, Social and Cultural Perspectives*, edited by Cynthia Chou and Geoffrey Benjamin, 7–76. Singapore: Institute of Southeast Asian Studies, 2001.

Bourdieu, Pierre. *Outline of a Theory of Practice.* Translated by Richard Nice. Cambridge: Cambridge University Press, 1977.

Bregel, Yuri. "Uzbeks, Qazaqs, and Turkmen." In *The Cambridge History of Inner Asia: The Chinggisid Age*, edited by Nicola Di Cosmo, Allen J. Frank, and Peter Golden, 221–236. Cambridge: Cambridge University Press, 2009.

Briggs, John. "Account of the Origin, History and Manners of the Race of Men called Bunjaras." In *Transactions of the Literary Society of Bombay* Vol. I.,170–197. London: Longman, Hurst, Rees, Orme, and Brown, 1819. Reprint, Bombay: Education Society's Press, 1877.

Bugeaud, Marechal. "La Guerre de Montagne II: La Kabylie." *Revue des Deux Mondes* (1829–1971), Nouvelle Priode 10, no. 2 (15 Avril, 1851): 225–274.

Burns, Robert, Lolita C. Baldor, and Matthew Lee. "Trump Defends Decision to Abandon Kurdish Allies in Syria." *AP News.* October 8, 2019. https://www.apnews.com/ac3115b4eb564288a03a5b8be868d2e5.

Celériér, J. "Chez Berbéres du Maroc." *Annales d'Histoire Economique et Sociale.* T.8, No. 39, (1936): 209–237.

Chatterjee, Indrani. *Forgotten Friends: Monks, Marriages, and Memories of Northeast India*. Delhi: Oxford University Press, 2013.

Chua, Amy. *Political Tribes: Group Instinct and the Fate of Nations*. New York: Penguin Books, 2018.

Crossley, Pamela Kyle. *A Translucent Mirror: History and Identity in Qing Imperial Ideology*. Berkeley: University of California Press, 1999.

———. Helen F. Siu, and Donald S. Sutton. *Empire at the Margins: Culture, Ethnicity, and Frontier in Early Modern China*. Berkeley: University of California Press, 2006.

———. *The Manchus*. Oxford: Blackwell Publishing, 1997.

de Jonnès, Moreau. "Recherches historiques sur les Caraïbes." *Journal des voyages, découvertes et navigations modernes* 2, no. 5 (1819): 5–27.

de Matos, Luís, ed. *Imagens do Oriente no século XVI*. Lisboa: Imprensa Nacional–Casa de Moeda, 1985.

de Rachewiltz, Igor. "The Secret History of the Mongols." *The Mongolia Society Bulletin* 9, no. 1 (16) (Spring, 1970): 55–69.

Dhal Samanta, Pranab. "3 months and a judge's panel make Gurjjars climb down." *Indian Express*. June 5, 2007. http://archive.indianexpress.com/news/3-months-and-a-judges-panel-make-gurjjars-climb-down/32764.

Di Cosmo, Nicola. *Ancient China and Its Enemies: The Rise of Nomadic Power in East Asian History*. Cambridge: Cambridge University Press, 2002.

———. Allen J. Frank and Peter B. Golden, eds. *The Cambridge History of Inner Asia: The Chinggisid Age*. Cambridge: Cambridge University Press, 2009.

Dikötter, Frank. "The Racialization of the Globe: An Interactive Interpretation." *Ethnic and Racial Studies* 31, no. 8, (2008): 1478–1496.

Dowd, Maureen. "Think Outside the Box Jack: Trump, Twitter and the society-crushing pursuit of monetized rage." *New York Times*, June 6, 2020. https://www.nytimes.com/2020/05/30/opinion/sunday/trump-twitter-jack-dorsey.html.

Ducuing, François. "La Guerre de Montagne II: La Kabylie. Marechal Bugeaud." *Revue des Deux Mondes* (1829–1971), Nouvelle Periode 10, no. 2 (15 Avril, 1851): 225–274.

Edgar, Adrienne. "Everyday Life among the Turkmen Nomads." In *Everyday Life in Central Asia: Past and Present*, edited by Jeff Sahadeo and Russell Zanca, 37–44. Bloomington: Indiana University Press, 2007.

Elliott, Mark. C. *The Manchu Way: The Eight Banners and Ethnic Identity in Late Imperial China*. Stanford: Stanford University Press, 2001.

Elphinstone, Mountstuart. *An Account of the Kingdom of Caubul and its Dependencies*. London: Richard Bentley, 1842.

Farra, Emily. "Which Street Style Tribe Did You Join in 2017?" *Vogue*, December 18, 2017. https://www.vogue.com/article/street-style-tribes-of-2017-top-trends-streetwear-demna-gvasalia-suits.

Ferdinand, Klaus. *Preliminary Notes on Hazara Culture*. *Historsk-filosofiske Meddelser*. Bind 37, no.5. Kobenhavn: Munksgaard, 1959.

Findlay, Carter V. *The Turks in World History*. New York: Oxford University Press, 2005.

Fiskesjö, Magnus. "On the 'Raw' and the 'Cooked' Barbarians of Imperial China." *Inner Asia* 1, no. 2 (1999): 139–168.

Forrest, George W., ed. *Selections from the Minutes and Other Official Writings of the Honorable Mounstuart Elphinstone*. London: Richard Bentley, 1884.

Forsyth, J. James. *The Highlands of Central India: Notes on Their Forests and Wild Tribes, Natural History, And Sports*. 2nd ed. London: Chapman & Hall, 1872.

Francois, Martin. *Memoires de Francois Martin, fondateur de Pondichery (1665–1696)*. Tome III. Paris: Societe de l'Histoire des Colonies Francaises, 1934.

Fried, Morton H. *The Evolution of Political Society: An Essay in Political Anthropology*. New York: Random House, 1967.

Fromherz, Allan J. *Ibn Khaldun: Life and Times*. Edinburgh: University of Edinburgh Press, 2010.

Gayer, George W. *Lectures on some Criminal Tribes of India* and *Religious Mendicants*. Nagpur: Publisher n/a, 1910. https://archive.org/stream/lecturesonsomecr00gayeuoft/lecturesonsomecr00gayeuoft_djvu.txt.

Geertz, Clifford. "The Integrative Revolution: Primordial Sentiments and Civil Politics in the New States." In *Old Societies and New States*, edited by Clifford Geertz, 105–157. New York: Free Press, 1963.

Goitein, S. D. *Jews and Arabs: Their Contacts through the Ages*. New York: Schocken Books, 1964.

Gold, Ann G. and Bhojuram Gujar, *In the Time of Trees and Sorrows: Nature, Power and Memory in Rajasthan*. Durham, NC: Duke University Press, 2002.

Golden, Peter. *An Introduction to the History of the Turkic Peoples: Ethnogenesis and State Formation in Medieval and Early Modern Eurasia and the Middle East*. Wiesbaden: Otto Harrassowitz, 1992.

———. "Ethnogenesis in the Tribal Zone: The Shaping of the Türks." *Archivum Eurasia Medii Aevi* 16 (2008–2009): 73–112.

Gommans, Jos. *The Rise of Indo-Afghan Empire, c. 1710–1780*. Indian edition. Delhi: Oxford University Press, 1999.

Gonzales, Roberto T. "Going 'Tribal': Notes on Pacification in the 21st Century." *Anthropology Today* 25, no. 2 (April 2009): 15–19.

Grinin, Leonid E. et al., eds. *The Early State, Its Alternatives and Analogues*. Volgograd: Uchitel, 2004.

Guha, Sumit. "Forest Polities and Agrarian Empires: The Khandesh Bhils c. 1700–1850." *Indian Economic and Social History Review* 33, no. 2 (1996): 133–153.

———. "Lower Strata, Older Races and Aboriginal Peoples: Racial Anthropology and Mythic History Past and Present." *Journal of Asian Studies* 57, no. 2 (1998): 423–441.

———. *Environment and Ethnicity in India, c. 1200–1991*. Cambridge: Cambridge University Press, 1999.

———. "States, Tribes, Castes: A Historical Re-exploration in Comparative Perspective." Special Article, *Economic and Political Weekly* 50, nos. 46–47 (November 2015): 50–57.

———. *History and Collective Memory in South Asia, 1200–2000*. Seattle: University of Washington Press, 2019.

Halperin, Charles J. "*Tsarev ulus*: Russia in the Golden Horde." *Cahiers du monde Russe et Soviétique* 23, no. 2 (1982): 257–263.

Hamalainen, Pekka. *The Comanche Empire*. New Haven: Yale University Press, 2008.

Hang, Lin. "Conquer and Govern: The Rise of the Jurchen and Their Jin Dynasty." In *Political Strategies of Identity-Building in Non-Han Empires in China*, edited by Francesca Fiaschetti and Julia Schneider, 35–57. Wiesbaden: Otto Harrassowitz, 2014.

Hassan, Hussein D. *Iraq: Tribal Structure, Social, and Political Activities*. Washington DC: Congressional report, 2007. https://apps.dtic.mil/dtic/tr/fulltext/u2/a464737.pdf.

Hassani, Ataollah. "Names and Appellations in the Shahsevan-e Baghdadi Confederacy." Special Issue: Nomads and Nomadism in Post-revolutionary Iran *Nomadic Peoples, New Series* 7, no. 2 (2003): 48–61.

Hopkins, Benjamin D. "The Frontier Crimes Regulation and Frontier Governmentality." *Journal of Asian Studies* 74, no. 2 (2015): 369–389.

———. *Ruling the Savage Periphery: Frontier Governance and the Making of the Modern State.* Cambridge MA: Harvard University Press, 2020.

Horowitz, Donald. *Ethnic Groups in Conflict.* 2nd ed. Berkeley: University of California Press, 2000.

Ibn Khaldun. *The Muqaddimah: An Introduction to History.* 3 vols. 2nd ed. Translated by Franz Rosenthal. Princeton: Princeton University Press, 1967.

Jackson, Peter. "The Mongol Age in Eastern Inner Asia." In *The Cambridge History of Inner Asia: The Chinggisid Age*, edited by Nicola Di Cosmo, Allen J. Frank, and Peter Golden, 26–45. Cambridge: Cambridge University Press, 2009.

Kakar, M. Hassan. *A Political and Diplomatic History of Afghanistan.* Leiden: Brill, 2006.

Keyes, Charles F. "Presidential Address: 'The Peoples of Asia'—Science and Politics in the Classification of Ethnic Groups in Thailand, China, and Vietnam." *Journal of Asian Studies* 61, no. 4 (2002): 1163–1204.

Khan, Ahsan Raza. *Chieftains in the Mughal Empire during the Reign of Akbar.* Simla: Indian Institute of Advanced Study, 1977.

Khazanov, A. M. "Myths and Paradoxes of Nomadism." *European Journal of Sociology* 22, no.1 (1981): 141–153.

———. *Nomads and the Outside World.* Translated by Julia Crookenden. Cambridge: Cambridge University Press, 1983.

———. "Nomads of the Eurasian Steppes in Historical Retrospective." In *The Early State, Its Alternatives and Analogues*, edited by Leonid E. Grinin et al., 476–500. Volgograd: Uchitel, 2004.

——— and André Wink, eds. *Nomads in the Sedentary World.* Richmond: Curzon, 2001.

Kingwell-Banham, Eleanor and Dorian Q. Fuller. "Shifting Cultivators in South Asia: Expansion, Marginalisation and Specialization." *Quaternary International* 249 (2012): 84–95.

La Raw, Maran. "On the Continuing Relevance of E. R. Leach's *Political Systems of Highland Burma* to Kachin Studies." In *Social Dynamics in the Highlands of Southeast Asia: Reconsidering Political Systems of Highland Burma by E. R. Leach,* edited by Francois Robinne and Mandy Sadan, 31–66. Leiden: Brill, 2007.

Lacher, Wolfram. "Families, Tribes and Cities in the Libyan Revolution." *Middle East Policy* XVIII, no. 4 (Winter 2011): 140–155.

Leach, Edmund R. *The Political Systems of Highland Burma: A Study of Kachin Social Structure.* London: G. Bell and Sons, 1954. Reprint, London: Athlone Press, 1990.

Leepracha, Prasit. "Becoming Indigenous Peoples in Thailand." *Journal of Southeast Asian Studies* 50, no. 1 (February 2019): 32–50.

Levi, Scott. "Turks and Tajiks in Central Asian History." In *Everyday Life in Central Asia: Past and Present,* edited by Jeff Sahadeo and Russell Zanca, 15–32. Bloomington: Indiana University Press, 2007.

Lindner, Rudi P. *Nomads and Ottomans in Medieval Anatolia.* Bloomington: Research Institute for Inner Asian Studies, 1983.

Mackintosh, James. *"Miscellaneous Works of the Right Honourable Sir James Mackintosh"* (Single volume edition, London: Longman, 1851).

Maître, Henri. *Les Régions Moï du Sud Indo-Chinois: Le Plateau du Darlac.* Paris: Plon, 1909.

Majumdar, Ramesh Chandra. *Corporate Life in Ancient India.* 3rd ed. Calcutta: Firma K. L. Mukhopadhyay, 1969.

Malcolm, John. *A Memoir of Central India, Including Malwa and Adjoining Provinces; with the History and Copious Illustrations of the Past and Present Condition of That Country.* New Delhi: Sagar Publications, 1970.

Masson Smith Jr., John. "Ayn Jalūt: Mamluk Success or Mongol Failure?" *Harvard Journal of Asiatic Studies* 44, no. 2 (Dec. 1984): 307–345.

May, Timothy. "Mongol Warfare in the Pre-Dissolution Period." *Golden Horde Review* 2, no. 1 (2015): 7–19.

McKinnon, Susan. "Domestic Exceptions: Evans-Pritchard and the Creation of Nuer Patrilineality and Equality." *Cultural Anthropology* 15, no. 1 (Feb. 2000): 35–83.

———. Sarah Turner, and Yann Roche. "Mapping Ethnic Diversity in Highland North Vietnam." *Geojournal* 57, no. 4 (2002): 281–299.

Michaud, Jean. *Historical Dictionary of the Peoples of the Southeast Asian Massif.* Lanham: Scarecrow Press, 2006.

Moens, S.M. *Report on the Settlement of the Bareilly District, North-Western Provinces.* Allahabad: North-Western Provinces Government Press, 1874.

Moodie, Megan. *We Were Adivasis: Aspiration in an Indian Scheduled Tribe.* Chicago: University of Chicago Press, 2015.

Mullaney, Thomas S. *Coming to Terms with the Nation: Ethnic Classification in Modern China*. Berkeley: University of California Press, 2011.

Munkh-Erdene, Lhamsuren. "Where Did the Mongol Empire Come From? Medieval Mongol Ideas of People, State and Empire." *Inner Asia* 13, no. 2 (2011): 211–237.

Nichols, Robert, ed. *The Frontier Crimes Regulation: A History in Documents*. Karachi: Oxford University Press, 2013.

Nicot, Jean. *Tresor de la Langue Francais* 1606. https://artflsrv03-uchicago.edu. ezproxy. lib.utexas.edu/philologic4/publicdicos/query?report=bibliography& head=tribu.

Obeyesekere, Gananath. "Colonial Histories and Vädda Primitivism: An Unorthodox Reading of Kandy Period Texts." *Art Sri Lanka*. Acessed September 4, 2020. www.artsrilanka.org/essays/vaddaprimitivism/index. html.

Olivelle, Patrick. *King, Governance and Law in Ancient India: Kauṭilya's Arthaśāstra*. South Asian Edition. New Delhi: Oxford University Press, 2013.

Onon, Urgunge, ed. and trans. *The Secret History of the Mongols: The Life and Times of Chinggis Khan*. Abingdon: Routledge Curzon, 2013.

Perdue, Peter C. *China Marches West: The Qing Conquest of Central Eurasia*. Cambridge: Belknap Press of Harvard University Press, 2005.

Pieke, Frank N. "Beyond Orthodoxy: Social and Cultural Anthropology in the People's Republic of China." In *Asian Anthropology*, edited by Jan Van Bremen, Eyal Ben-Ari, and Syed Farid Alatas, 59–79. Routledge: London 2004.

Radhakrishna, Meena. *Dishonoured by History: "Criminal Tribes" and British Colonial Policy*. Hyderabad: Orient Longman, 2001.

"Rajasthan assembly passes quota bill, Gujjars call off stir." *India Today*. February 13, 2019. https://www.indiatoday.in/india/story/rajasthan-government-five-per-cent-quota-bill-gujjars-four-castes-1455070-2019-02-13.

Rehmann, J. and M. Friéville. "État politique et militaire des Khalkas-Mongols." *Journal des voyages, découvertes et navigations modernes* 2, no. 5 (1819): 27–51.

Rhoads, Edward J. M. *Manchus and Han: Ethnic Relations and Political Power in Late Qing and Early Republican China, 1861–1928*. Seattle: University of Washington Press, 2000.

Roy-Burman, B. K. *The Siddis: An Ethnographic Study*. Delhi: Manager of Publications, 1969.

Sadan, Mandy, ed. *Being and Becoming Kachin: Histories beyond the State in the Borderworlds of Burma*. Oxford: Oxford University Press, 2013.

Salemink, Oscar. *The Ethnography of Vietnam's Central Highlanders: A Historical Contextualization 1850–1970*. London: Routledge Curzon, 2003.

"Samuel." Accessed May 29, 2020. https://www.kingjamesbibleonline.org/1-Samuel-Chapter-8/.

Sarkar, Jadunath. *Persian Records of Maratha History: Delhi Affairs 1761–1788*. Bombay: Director of Archives, Government of Bombay, 1953.

Scoones, Ian. "New Ecology and the Social Sciences: What Prospects for a Fruitful Engagement?" *Annual Review of Anthropology* 28, no. 1 (1999): 479–507.

Scott, James C. *The Art of Not Being Governed: An Anarchist History of Upland Southeast Asia*. New Haven: Yale University Press, 2009.

———. *Against the Grain: A Deep History of the Earliest States*. New Haven: Yale University Press, 2017.

Service, Elman R. "The Mind of Lewis H. Morgan [and Comments and Reply]." *Current Anthropology* 22, no. 1 (Feb. 1981): 25–43.

Sinor, Denis, ed. *The Cambridge History of Early Inner Asia*. Cambridge: Cambridge University Press, 1990.

Soudavar, Abolala. "The Early Safavids and their cultural interactions with surrounding states." In *Iran and the Surrounding World*, edited by Nikki R. Kedie and Rudi Matthee, 89-120. Seattle: University of Washington Press, 2002.

Srinivas, M.N. "Caste in Modern India." *The Journal of Asian Studies* 16, no. 4 (Aug., 1957): 529–548.

Sundar, Nandini ed. *The Scheduled Tribes and Their India: Politics, Identities, Policies and Work*. Delhi: Oxford University Press, 2016.

Szonyi, Michael. *Practicing Kinship: Lineage and Descent in Late Imperial China*. Stanford: Stanford University Press, 2002.

———. *The Art of Being Governed: Everyday Politics in Late Imperial China*. Princeton: Princeton University Press, 2017.

Tambiah, Stanley J. "The Galactic Polity: The Structure of Traditional Kingdoms in Southeast Asia." *Annals of the New York Academy of Sciences* 293, no. 1 (1977): 69–97.

Tapper, Richard. "The Tribes in Eighteenth- and Nineteenth-Century Iran." In *The Cambridge History of Iran*, Vol. 7, edited by Peter Avery, Gavin R.G. Hambly and C. Melville, 506–541. Cambridge: Cambridge University Press, 1991.

———. *Frontier Nomads of Iran: A Political History of the Shahsevan*. Cambridge: Cambridge University Press, 1997.

Tone, William H. *Some Particular Institutions of the Maratta People* (London: Reprinted for J. Derrett, 1799).

Trautmann, Thomas. *Kautilya and the Arthsasastra: A Statistical Investigation of the Authorship and Evolution of the Text*. Leiden: E. J. Brill, 1971.

"Tribus." *A Latin Dictionary*. http://www.perseus.tufts.edu/hopper/text?doc=Perseus:text:1999.04.0059:entry=tribus.

Twitchett, Denis Crispin and John King Fairbank, eds. *The Cambridge History of China*. Cambridge: Cambridge University Press, 1978.

——— and Michael Loewe, eds. *The Cambridge History of China: The Ch'in and Han Empires, 221 BC–AD 220*. Cambridge: Cambridge University Press, 1986.

Upham, Steadman, ed. *The Evolution of Political Systems*. Cambridge: Cambridge University Press, 1990.

Vad, G. C. compiled. *Selections from the Satara Raja's and Peshwa Diaries*. 8 Parts. Poona: Deccan Vernacular Translation Society, 1902–1911.

Verghese, B. G. *India's Northeast Resurgent: Ethnicity, Insurgency, Governance and Development*. New Delhi: Konark Publishers for the Centre for Policy Research, 1996.

von Fürer-Haimendorf, Christoph. *Tribes of India: The Struggle for Survival*. Berkeley: University of California Press, 1982.

Walshe, Maurice, trans. *The Long Discourses of the Buddha, a Translation of the Digha Nikaya*. Boston: Wisdom Publications, 2005.

Wittfogel, Karl. *Oriental Despotism. A Comparative Study of Total Power*. New Haven: Yale University Press, 1958.

Wood, John R. "India's Narmada River Dams: Sardar Sarovar under Siege." *Asian Survey* 33, no. 10 (Oct. 1993): 968–984.